The

ULTIMATE
MAKEOVER

The
ULTIMATE
MAKEOVER

becoming spiritually beautiful in Christ

Sharon Jaynes

355ว
MOODY PUBLISHERS
CHICAGO

All Scripture quotations, unless otherwise indicated, are taken from the *Holy Bible, New International Version®*. NIV®. Copyright © 1973, 1978, 1984 by International Bible Society. Used by permission of Zondervan Publishing House. All rights reserved.

Scripture quotations marked NASB are taken from the *New American Standard Bible®*, Copyright © The Lockman Foundation 1960, 1962, 1963, 1968, 1971, 1972, 1973, 1975, 1977, 1995. Used by permission.

Scripture quotations marked NLT are taken from the *Holy Bible, New Living Translation*, copyright © 1996. Used by permission of Tyndale House Publishers, Inc., Wheaton, Illinois 60189. All rights reserved.

Scripture quotations marked KJV are taken from the King James Version.

Scripture quotations marked AMP are taken from the *Amplified Bible, Old Testament*, copyright © 1965, 1987 by The Zondervan Corporation. The *Amplified Bible, New Testament*, copyright © 1954, 1958, 1987 by The Lockman Foundation. Used by permission.

Cover Photography: ©2002 Stone/Kaz Chiba

Cover: Ragont Design

Library of Congress Cataloging-in-Publication Data

Jaynes, Sharon.
    The ultimate makeover : becoming beautiful from the inside out / by Sharon Jaynes.
        p. cm.
    ISBN 0-8024-3556-4
    1. Christian women--Religious life. I. Title.

BV4527 .J395 2003
248.8'43--dc21

2002013685

1 3 5 7 9 10 8 6 4 2

Printed in the United States of America

*Dedicated to one of the most beautiful women I have ever known,
whose love for the Lord radiates both inside and out*
—Lysa TerKeurst

CONTENTS

ACKNOWLEDGMENTS

I am forever grateful for the many people who made this book possible.

The four people who started me on this journey of understanding my true identity in Christ: Bill and Annabel Gillham, Neil Anderson, and my mentor and friend Mary Marshall Young.

The wonderful Moody Press team for catching the vision of Proverbs 31 Ministries and enabling us to touch women's hearts through the written word: Greg Thornton, Bill Thrasher, Elsa Mazon, and Dave DeWit. Cheryl Dunlop for her editing expertise. Janis Backing, Rhonda Elfstrand, and John Hinkley for spreading the word.

The incredible staff of Proverbs 31 Ministries: Lysa TerKeurst, Joel Bennett, Lisa Britt, Shelly Chen, Ann Conway, Cheri Jimenez, Suzi Kallam, Charlene Kidd, Sherry Killion,

Marie Ogram, Laurie Webster, and Glynnis Whitwer. You are truly a chandelier of Christ's light, each one uniquely brilliant, yet unified to shine the light as one.

The many friends who have encouraged and prayed for me during this project: Linda Butler, Gayle Montgomery, Lisa Thomas, Naomi Gingerich, Heidi Hershberger, KC Lynn, and Sarah Fulmer.

My mother, Louise Edwards, who prays for me from a distance.

The many friends who have shared their lives with me and allowed me to tell others their stories in the pages of this book.

My wonderful husband, Steve, who has endured stacks of paper, late nights with me at the computer, and "Honey, can you read this one more time?"

INTRODUCTION

I remember as a little girl sneaking into my mother's closet and slipping my child-size feet into her size seven high heels. I'd also stand on my tiptoes on a chair, pull a hat off the top shelf, and plop it on my head like an oversized lampshade. Her satin evening jacket with sleeves that hung eight inches below my fingertips gave a nice elegant touch to my outfit. A lady going to a party would never be caught without "putting on her face," so I crept into the bathroom, opened the forbidden drawer, and created a clownish work of art on the palette of my face. Red rouge circles on my cheeks, heaps of blue eye shadow on my munchkin lids, and smeared orange lipstick far exceeding the proper borders were finished off with a dusting of facial powder with an oversized brush.

From the time a little girl stretches on her tiptoes to

◆ ◆

get a peek in the mirror, she desires to be beautiful—perhaps like her mommy. As the girl moves into the teen years, she experiments with makeup, delves into fashion, and attempts various hairstyles. Then it's on to makeover ideas in magazines and on talk shows. If one idea doesn't work—well, there's always next month.

I've always dreamed about spending a day at a spa and walking out a brand new person. After all, Queen Esther stayed in a spa for an entire year before she claimed her title of Mrs. Xerxes. Her beauty regimen included six months with oils of myrrh and six months with perfumes and cosmetics (Esther 2:12). Not only that, she was assigned seven maids to take care of her. Now that sounds like a spa package worth looking into!

Let's face it, women want to be beautiful. However, many fail to realize that beauty—true beauty—begins on the inside and works its way out.

But how do you become beautiful on the inside? You will not discover the secret in magazines, on talk shows, or in secular self-help books. Becoming beautiful from the inside out is a feat only God can accomplish in you. He has issued each and every one of us a VIP gift certificate at His heavenly spa to experience the *ultimate makeover*. He doesn't just cover up our flaws; He miraculously starts from scratch and makes us new. He even gives us new names to go with our new look—children of God, salt of the earth, precious and dearly loved.

God's ultimate makeover also includes an exercise plan as we learn to run like Paul—forgetting what lies behind and pressing on toward the goal of becoming more like Christ. An added benefit of the exercise regimen is the spiritual weight loss, which comes when we release our burdens and worries to God. For those who are concerned with worry lines, we'll see how to have a faith-lift as we let go of fear and learn to trust. And we'll do some exfoliation to slough away unsightly old habits and unhealthy thought patterns. This makeover also includes a wardrobe change that puts you in a power suit while maintaining the gracious elegance of a princess.

At the end of this book, you'll find a Bible study to help you if you want to go deeper into God's Word. The study can be used as your own personal beauty treatment or in a group as you grow and glow together.

I was fourteen years old when I experienced a spiritual makeover by accepting Jesus Christ as my Savior. At that time, a new, fully alive, eternal spirit that I inherited from Christ replaced my old dead one that I inherited from Adam. However, it wasn't until almost twenty years later that I realized I was a child of the King but had been living like a pauper.

When I think of the word *makeover*, I think of the prefix "re." "Re" attached to the front of a word means "to do again." God is a God of "do overs." He takes all our ugliness and remakes us into the image of Christ. Here, in *Ultimate Makeover*, I want to introduce you to the God who realizes our weakness, receives us just as we are, reclaims what the Enemy stole from us, refills our empty places, refreshes us with His mercies, refines our rough edges, releases us from bondage, renews our minds, and replaces beauty for ashes. Along the way, we'll meet many women who have tried God's beauty tips with glowing results.

Your appointment has been made. God is waiting. Let's get started!

A MAKEOVER, PLEASE!

Uncovering the Real Problem

THE MOST BEAUTIFUL WOMAN

A successful beauty product company asked the people in a large city to send pictures along with brief letters about the most beautiful women they knew. Within a few weeks thousands of letters were delivered to the company.

One letter in particular caught the attention of the employees, and soon it was handed to the company president. The letter was written by a young boy who was obviously from a broken home and living in a run-down neighborhood. With spelling corrections, an excerpt from his letter said: "This beautiful woman lives down the street from me. I visit her every day. She makes me feel like the most important kid in the world. We play checkers and she listens to my problems. She understands me and when I leave she always yells out the door that she's proud of me."

The boy ended his letter saying, "This picture shows you that she is the most beautiful woman. I hope I have a wife as pretty as her."

Intrigued by the letter, the president asked to see this woman's picture. His secretary handed him a photograph of a smiling, toothless woman, well advanced in years, sitting in a wheelchair. Sparse gray hair was pulled back in a bun. Wrinkles that formed deep furrows on her face were somehow diminished by the twinkle in her eyes.

"We can't use this woman," explained the president, smiling. "She would show the world that our products aren't necessary to be beautiful."[1]

This little boy had discovered a valuable truth. Beauty—true beauty—begins on the inside and works its way out.

Americans spend more than seven billion dollars a year on cosmetics. Magazine racks bulge each month with periodicals offering dramatic makeovers for women of every shape, color, and size. They tell us how to thin thighs, firm flab, tuck in tummies, build biceps, tighten tushes, lengthen lashes, whiten teeth, and plump lips. We can learn the proper way to apply makeup, choose the best hairstyles to frame and flatter facial shapes, and determine what color wardrobe is best for our particular skin tone. Cosmetic surgery procedures among women have increased by a dramatic 165 percent since 1992.[2]

The obsession with outward appearance isn't limited to older women fighting the effects of aging and gravity who have expendable income. In the year 2000, American youths spent $155 billion on beauty products and trips to salons and spas—largely financed by willing parents.[3]

Talk show hosts' most popular programs have been on makeovers. Viewers love to watch an artist transform a frumpy middle-aged housewife into a sophisticated cosmopolitan with just a snip of the scissors, a stroke of blush, and an updated wardrobe. Silently we wonder, *Could that ever be me?*

I'm not saying I've never read the makeover articles in the magazines or tried a few of their suggestions. But I do know this: No number of skin creams, makeup, designer clothes, or exercise regimens will make a woman truly beautiful, for true beauty is an outward reflection of an inward glow. Rosalind Russell said, "Taking joy in life is a woman's best cosmetic."

Cheap Nails

One of the greatest philosophers of all time is Charlie Brown, the little round-headed kid in Charles Schulz's *Peanuts* cartoon. But even Charlie Brown has his problems. In one strip, Charlie Brown is standing at Lucy's psychiatric booth getting a little helpful advice. Lucy says, "Don't build your house on the sand, Charlie Brown." Then a gust of wind comes and blows Lucy, Charlie, and her booth up into the air, to land in a crumpled heap. In the final frame she concludes, "Or use cheap nails."

I see many women today who have started building their spiritual houses on the solid rock of Jesus Christ, but then proceed to build on that foundation with the cheap nails of outward appearance, performance, possessions, power, and the praises of others. Alas, when the strong winds of adversity begin to blow, just like Lucy's makeshift psychiatric booth, they fall apart.

In 1 Corinthians 3:10–15, Paul talks about two types of building materials. One type is wood, hay, and straw. These are what man produces. They are very temporary and can be burnt up or lost in a moment. The other type of building material is gold, silver, and precious stones. God has created them, but we have to discover them—which sometimes requires us to dig through mounds of dirt.

The modern culture's ideas on how to experience a makeover

are very temporary, but the Word of God's truths are eternal with lasting results. We can try the beauty tips in the magazines, but true beauty occurs when we sit in God's spa and let Him perform a miracle.

Before we begin with the ultimate makeover, we need to get to the root of the problem: Why are we so ugly in the first place? How did we get into this fix?

The Root of the Problem

Several years ago I owned a car that continually overheated. The first time I saw the little red needle pointing to the big "H" on the dashboard, I assumed it meant the car was hot. It was in the middle of August and, frankly, I was hot too, so I wasn't terribly alarmed. I decided to mosey on down to the dealership about twelve miles away to have it checked out. Big mistake.

After about a minute or so, steam began billowing from under the hood, the engine began knocking angrily, and the little engine that could decided it couldn't any longer. It died in the middle of a busy intersection on a Friday afternoon in 5:00 traffic. The car was towed to the dealership where the mechanic delivered the unfortunate news.

"Mrs. Jaynes, you see that needle that is pointing to the 'H'?" the repairman asked. "That means that the engine is runnin' hot. When you see that, you've got to stop right away. Since you kept goin', you burned up your engine. It's a goner. You'll have to get a new one."

"That sounds expensive," I moaned.

"Oh, it'll be about four thousand dollars," he answered, while continuing to poke around under the hood.

Four thousand dollars! And all because I didn't stop the car when it overheated . . . all because I didn't heed the warning signs. It was a painful lesson.

I got a new engine, and you can imagine my alarm when I noticed that little red needle pointing to "H" a few weeks later. This time, I stopped right away. Once again, my car was towed to the dealership. Once again, they made adjustments, gave reassurances, and sent me on my way.

Over the following weeks, my car overheated three times. Each time, it was towed to the shop and the mechanic made adjustments. Finally, I said "no more" and got rid of the car.

The trouble was, the mechanic never fixed the cause of the problem, but only tinkered with the symptoms. He fixed first one thing and then another, but never got to the root of the problem to find out why the car was overheating in the first place.

How like us. We continue to tinker, fixing one flaw and then another, but never getting to the root of the problem. Many times when reading the Bible, we tend to skip over the doctrinal sections and run to the practical sections. We want the "how tos" without the "why fors." In this age of instant messaging, microwave cooking, and fax machines, we want a quick fix without understanding the deep truths of Scripture. We say, "Just tell me what to do and I'll do it." "Give me a ten-step program, and I'll check the steps off one by one. Just tell me how to be beautiful from the inside out, and I'll add it to my to-do list." But in order to experience the ultimate makeover, we must begin with ultimate truth.

Before we begin this journey let's go back and do a little genetic research to find out why we need a spiritual makeover in the first place. Doctors require their patients to fill out a questionnaire called a "health history" because the medical field has determined that certain illnesses have genetic tendencies. If your grandmother had diabetes, then you are more at risk for the same disease. If your father had heart disease, you are more likely to have it as well.

In having an ultimate makeover, we must also look back at our parentage; however, I believe that if we want to get to the root of the problem, we must go back further than a few generations. We've got to go all the way back to the Garden—to the beginning of time.

THE REAL PROBLEM

A preacher once said, "Your problem is that you don't know what the problem is. You think your problem is your problem, but that's not the problem at all. Your problem is not your problem, and that's your main problem." To determine the real problem, we need to go back to the Garden of Eden. As Julie Andrews sang in the *Sound of Music*, "Let's start at the very beginning, a very good place to start."

In the beginning God created the heavens and the earth. I never tire of reading Genesis chapter one and imagining the birth of the universe and all it contains. On the first day He created light. Then He created the sky to separate the water on earth from the water in heaven. He gathered the water together to form the sea and let dry ground appear to form land. He caused the land to produce vegetation and created the sun to govern the day and the moon and stars to govern the night. He stocked the seas with living creatures and the sky with birds. On the fifth day, God created all living creatures that move along the ground.

But something was missing. God wanted something more. On the sixth day, God said, "Let us make man in our image" (Genesis 1:26). Then "the LORD God formed the man from the dust of the ground and breathed into his nostrils the breath of life, and the man became a living being" (2:7). The word *formed* is the same word used for a potter as he forms a vessel with clay. What a beautiful picture as we see God lovingly shaping and molding Adam's most intricate parts with His fingertips and breathing the very breath of God into his lungs.

After each day of creation, as the sun set over the horizon, God looked at His handiwork and said, "It is good." The one exception was when He said, "It is *not good* for the man to be alone" (Genesis 2:18, italics added).

> But for Adam no suitable helper was found. So the LORD God caused the man to fall into a deep sleep; and while he was sleeping, he took one of the man's ribs and closed up the place with flesh. Then the LORD God made a woman from the rib he had taken out of the man, and he brought her to the man. (Genesis 2:20-22)

The *New American Standard Bible* says God "fashioned" Eve. He took extra special care when He created you. He "fashioned" woman, and we've been interested in fashion ever since!

Up to this point, Adam had been silent. However, when God presented him with Eve, I imagine he said, "Whoa! Now *this* is good!" (Hence, "whoa, man—a woman.") We don't know that for sure, but we do know that Adam's first recorded words were upon seeing Eve. "This is now bone of my bones and flesh of my flesh; she shall be called 'woman,' for she was taken out of man" (Genesis 2:23).

All was well in the Garden—for a while.

Three Parts of Man*

I recall my kindergarten teacher saying, "Class, this year we are going to learn our ABCs and 123s." Everything else I learned over the next sixteen years of formal education was built on that foundation. In order to truly understand how to experience the ultimate makeover, we are going to have to go back and review some

---

*For the rest of this book, when I use the word "man," I am referring to "mankind," meaning both male and female.

of the basic 123s. As we've already discovered, you can't solve a problem if you don't understand what the real problem is.

The Bible explains God as a triune Being: God the Father, God the Son, and God the Holy Spirit. All three were present at Creation. God said, "Let *us* make man in *our* image." When He created Adam and Eve in His image, He created them in three parts as well: body, soul, and spirit (1 Thessalonians 5:23).

In order to visualize the three parts of man, let's think about the three parts of an apple. The peeling represents the body, the pulp represents the soul, and the seeds or the core represents the spirit. The body (peeling) is the part we see. Our earthly body is temporary and only exists for a short period of time. Paul refers to our body as a "tent" or a temporary dwelling, and he also mentions a future heavenly body (2 Corinthians 5:1–4). Some refer to our body as an "earth suit." It is the vehicle through which a soul interacts with the environment and other people. The body encompasses our five senses: sight, touch, taste, smell, and hearing. The body by itself is not the man, because man can exist apart from his earthly body. As one inexperienced preacher said while standing by the casket at his first funeral, "What we have here is an empty shell. The nut has already left us!"

We also have a soul. The soul houses the mind, will, and emotions. It allows us to think, choose, and feel emotions. The brain is part of the body, but the mind is part of the soul. The mind uses the brain to function, much like you use a computer to perform certain tasks. The mind is not the brain, but the seat of our personality. The soul determines the personality. Some commentators only note that we are material and immaterial, or body and spirit/soul. However, others believe we are in three parts. Although there are convincing arguments on both sides, I tend to believe we are three: body, soul, and spirit. The writer of Hebrews notes, "The word of God is living and active. Sharper than any double-edged sword, it penetrates even to dividing soul and spirit, joints and marrow; it judges the thoughts and attitudes of the heart" (Hebrews 4:12).

There is nothing worse than purchasing a beautiful, highly polished red delicious apple and biting into it only to find it mealy and

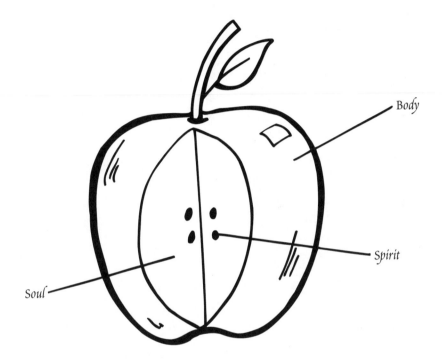

mushy on the inside. Well, maybe there is something worse—a beautiful woman who opens her mouth to reveal a harsh, cruel, cold soul on the inside. Solomon says that's like putting a "gold ring in a pig's snout" (Proverbs 11:22a). What a waste.

Becky experienced this firsthand when she was nineteen years old. She was performing as a runway model at her hometown department store. She was 5′2″ and 100 pounds, just the perfect size to model apparel from the petite department. But she had always longed to be tall and slender like the runway models from the big cities. On one occasion, the management of the store where

Becky worked flew in a New York model to add to the excitement of a fashion show event. Becky was thrilled to watch a professional perform with poise and elegance.

Becky explained, "I can remember standing behind a rack of clothes and peering admiringly as the 5′8″ sleek blonde glided up and down the runway with the grace and poise of a queen. 'Oh God,' I prayed, 'how I wish I could be like her.'"

After the fashion show was over Becky was gathering her belongings from backstage when she overheard the model in a fit of rage.

"I don't even know what happened," Becky said. "All I know is that this beautiful woman who I had so admired, almost worshiped, was spewing the filthiest language I had ever heard and slinging clothes and shoes all around the room. I ran out of the store and cried all the way home. Disappointment and disillusionment filled my heart. 'Oh God,' I prayed once again, 'please don't ever let me be like her.'"

Becky had learned that nothing is more disappointing than a beautiful apple that is mealy inside—unless, of course, it is one that is rotten to the core.

The core of man is the spirit. While our present body is temporal, the spirit is eternal. Paul said, "To be absent from the body [is to] be present with the Lord" (2 Corinthians 5:8 KJV). Paul knew that when his body was no more, his spirit would live for eternity in heaven with God. Just as the body is necessary for people to relate to one another, the spirit is necessary for man to relate to God.

In the apple model, the seeds in the core represent the spirit. Just as the seeds determine the type of apple (e.g., Granny Smith, Red Delicious, Rome), the spirit determines a person's true identity. "For you have been born again, not of perishable seed, but of imperishable, through the living and enduring word of God" (1 Peter 1:23). The Bible states that there are two types of "seed" that determine if you are a good apple or a bad apple. One is perishable and one is imperishable. We will take a look at the two different types in just a moment.

At Creation, Adam and Eve were made in the image of God and perfect in every way. Their bodies had no genetic defects or flaws, their souls were naked and unashamed, and their spirits were in perfect union with God—two prize apples!

Three Aspects of Life

Man was created in three parts, and he was alive in every area. "The Lord God formed the man from the dust of the ground and breathed into his nostrils the breath of life, and the man became a living being" (Genesis 2:7). The best description of the word *life* is found in the Greek forms of the word. We have one word for "love," but the Greeks had three: *agape* (unconditional Christlike love), *phileo* (brotherly love), and *eros* (sexual love). Likewise, we have one word for "life," but the Greeks had three: *bios, psyche,* and *zoe.*

1. *Bios* is the life of the body. (This is where we get the word *biosphere.*)
2. *Psyche* is the life of the soul: mind, will, and emotions. (This is where we get the word psychology.)
3. *Zoe* is the life of the spirit.

Adam and Eve were fully alive in all three dimensions. Their bodies, souls, and spirits were in complete communion with God.

Three Glowing Attributes

Adam and Eve had no unmet needs. Instead of needs, they had three glowing attributes.

1. Significance: Adam and Eve had great significance as rulers of all the creatures over the entire earth. They had an important job to do.
2. Safety and Security: Adam and Eve were very secure in their relationship with God. All their needs were cared for.
3. Belonging: Adam and Eve were content. They were in perfect union with God and each other. They had a sense of belonging.

Three Temptations

Adam and Eve had a wonderfully fulfilling life. God was right there with them at all times. He walked and talked with them in the cool of the day and met all of their needs.

> I give you every seed-bearing plant on the face of the whole earth and every tree that has fruit with seed in it. They will be yours for food. And to all the beasts of the earth and all the birds of the air and all the creatures that move on the ground—everything that has the breath of life in it—I give every green plant for food. (Genesis 1:29)

He gave only one restriction. "You are free to eat from any tree in the garden; but you must not eat from the tree of the knowledge of good and evil, for when you eat of it you will surely die" (Genesis 2:16–17).

In Genesis 3, we see where our ancestors made a grave decision that affected every person born thereafter. Satan came to Eve in the form of a serpent and tempted her with the one restriction placed on her by God.

1. He questioned God. "Did God really say, 'You must not eat from any tree in the garden'?"

2. He denied God. "You will not surely die!" the serpent said to the woman.

3. He caused her to doubt God's justice. "For God knows that when you eat of it your eyes will be opened, and you will be like God, knowing good and evil."

Satan is the great deceiver who takes what worked in the Garden and continues to use the same tactics today. He is not very creative, but he is highly effective. It is very important to understand his tactics in order to recognize and defeat them. Paul said he was not ignorant of his schemes (2 Corinthians 2:11 NASB), and we shouldn't be either. Satan tempts us to question God. *Has God said you must stay married to a man who doesn't meet your needs?* He tempts us to deny God. *God wouldn't count it as a sin for you to seek happiness elsewhere.* He tempts us to doubt God's justice. *What kind of God is He who would deny you the right to find happiness in the arms of a different man who appreciates you?*

This is Satan's battle plan, and his desire is to catch us off guard. Let's consider the following possible scenario about a woman we'll call Anna.

He attacked Anna when she least expected it. She was a beautiful woman who loved opera and the stage. She had an incredible voice, and when she sang in church, it was as though she were ushering the congregation right into the throne room of God. In her single years, she had had aspirations of joining an opera company, but she put those dreams on hold to settle down with the man of her dreams. She and Rob had no children, but they were content and very much in love.

One night, while enjoying a romantic dinner at a restaurant with her husband, she struck up a conversation with their waitress. It seems the waitress was auditioning for an opera the next day and was a bit nervous. The mention of an opera audition piqued Anna's interest, and she inquired further.

"An opera?" she asked. "Which one?"

Rob knew the particular opera the waitress mentioned. It was about the tumultuous life of a prostitute. He watched as Anna grew animated with excitement about the possibility of auditioning herself. He voiced his concerns about the sordid theme of the said opera, but Anna ignored his questions.

Enter Satan. I envision him whispering in her ear: "Anna, this is what you've always wanted—a chance to get back on stage again. So what if the theme is a bit off color. It's art! God hasn't said not to do such operas. It's not in the Bible. Rob is just being overprotective. Besides, he knows you might be successful, and he's probably just jealous. Who knows, you might even be able to witness to the cast. Besides, you deserve this chance."

"Oh, Rob," Anna said, "God doesn't mind me being in this opera. It's art, and besides, maybe I will be able to witness to the cast!"

"I don't feel good about this," Rob argued. "Participating in an opera with this type of story line can't be honoring to God."

Enter Satan: "It's not going to hurt you to try out. You might not get the part anyway. Besides, Rob's being controlling. Aren't you your own woman? Are you going to let a man tell you what you can and can't do?"

"Rob, it's no big deal," Anna countered. "I might not get a part anyway. Besides, you're being controlling. I'm strong enough to handle this."

"Even so," Rob answered, "just know that I do not want you to do this."

The romantic dinner was over.

Two weeks later, Anna auditioned for the opera and secured the female lead—that of a prostitute. Satan had slithered his way into the cracked door and wedged himself in the crack. Anna sang more passionately than ever before, flaunted her risquély dressed body across the stage, and enjoyed the kisses of her leading man. Rob watched helplessly as his wife became another woman before his very eyes, both on and off stage.

Three weeks after the close of the opera, while Rob was gone to the grocery store, Anna packed up her belongings and left, never to return. It seems she had a new leading man.

Satan grinned and made another check mark on his victory board.

Dear sister, do not be deceived. Satan is a liar and the father of lies. He still tells lies today. He still deceives those who will listen in the same way he deceived Eve. He tempted her in the three areas of her being, and he tempts us there as well.

"When the woman saw that the fruit of the tree was . . .

1. "Good for food"—her body
2. "Pleasing to the eye"—her soul (mind, will, and emotions)
3. "And also desirable for gaining wisdom"—her spirit (she believed the lie that if she ate from this tree, she would be like God)

". . . she took [the fruit] and ate it. She also gave some to her husband, who was with her, and he ate it. Then the eyes of both of them were opened, and they realized they were naked; so they sewed fig leaves together and made coverings for themselves" (Genesis 3:6–7). At that moment shame entered the world and their relationship with God was broken. They were banished from God's presence and cast out of the garden with cherubim waving flaming swords to prevent them from entering again (vv. 23–24).

Do you remember God's penalty for eating from the tree of the knowledge of good and evil? The punishment was death. The question arises, Did they die? This is where so many have missed a vital truth. *Yes, they did die.* Their bodies did not die right away, even though the process was set into motion. However, at that very moment of disobedience, their spirits died. Their *zoe* life was taken away, and every person who has been born since that time has been born with a living body but a dead spirit. "Therefore, just as sin entered the world through one man, and death through sin, and in this way death came to all men, because all sinned" (Romans 5:12; see also 1 Corinthians 15:21–22; Ephesians 2:1). While most think of the penalty as being cast out of the Garden, the real penalty was spiritual death.

Think back to the apple model for a moment. If the seed of an apple were to go bad, the entire apple would suffer as well. Adam and Eve's "seed" or spirit died, and they became rotten to the core. But God didn't leave man that way. In *The Gift for All People*, Max Lucado gives the hope of the promise in the Garden: "The moment the forbidden fruit touched the lips of Eve, the shadow of the cross appeared on the horizon. And between that moment and the moment the man with the mallet placed the spike against the wrist of God, a master plan was fulfilled."

One night, a Pharisee named Nicodemus came to Jesus and wanted to know more about His teachings. Jesus told him, "I tell you the truth, no one can enter the kingdom of God unless he is born again."

Nicodemus was confused and asked, "Surely he cannot enter a second time into his mother's womb to be born!"

Jesus answered, "I tell you the truth, no one can enter the kingdom of God unless he is born of water and the Spirit. Flesh gives birth to flesh, but the Spirit gives birth to spirit. You should not be surprised at my saying, 'You must be born again.' The wind blows wherever it pleases. You hear its sound, but you cannot tell where it comes from or where it is going. So it is with everyone born of the Spirit" (John 3:5–8).

Jesus was telling Nicodemus that in order for a person to enter heaven, he or she must have a new birth of the Spirit. Why? Because our spirit, our *zoe* life, was destroyed when Adam and Eve chose to disobey, so we must be spiritually born again.

Christ is not interested in religious people with dead spirits. He's interested in alive spirits who worship Him in spirit and in truth.

The Three Glaring Needs

Before the Fall, Eve felt significant, safe, and secure and had a sense of belonging. She was perfect and complete, lacking nothing. However, after she disobeyed God, her *zoe* life was taken away and her glowing attributes became glaring needs.

1. Eve lost her sense of significance and felt shame.
2. Eve lost her sense of safety and security and felt fear.
3. Eve lost her sense of belonging and felt emptiness and rejection.

She tried wearing a new outfit, but that didn't cover her feelings of insecurity. She tried hiding so no one would notice her imperfections, but she forgot that God sees everything. She even tried having a few kids to fill the emptiness and reverse the feelings of rejection, but their failures only accentuated her inadequacies. No matter what she tried, Eve's glaring needs were blinding. She was ugly from the inside out and rotten to the core.

And this brings us to the real problem—the reason we need an ultimate makeover. Our glaring needs mask the beauty that God intended for each and every one of His children. God desires for us to turn to Him and allow our needs for significance, safety, and security to be met in Jesus Christ. Satan desires for us to attempt to get those needs met in our own way and by our own strength. Our dead spirits and sinful nature cause darkness and ugliness to rule in our hearts and minds, but Jesus can make us beautiful. He is the makeover artist.

Gin was a woman who experienced the makeover power of Jesus Christ. She came to America from Korea in search of a better, more prosperous life. In order to adjust as quickly as possible to the new culture, she registered for an English language class at the local air force base. A corporal who taught the class became enamored by this beautiful, petite "doll" from Korea. After a few months, they fell in love and were married.

Gin's new husband took her to a church service one Sunday, and for the first time she heard the story of Creation, the Fall of man, the resulting sin nature to all mankind, and the redemptive power of Jesus Christ to save us and make us new.

She went home that evening and looked in the mirror. Gin was horrified at what she saw. In halting English, Gin explained. "When I looked in the mirror, I looked ugly. My face was dark and dirty. I could see sin. I had never noticed before, but the sin made me ugly."

The next week, Gin went back to church. When the pastor gave the altar call at the close of the service, Gin ran forward and accepted Jesus Christ as her Lord and Savior.

"After I accepted Christ, I went back home and looked in the mirror again. Now I was beautiful. The sin and darkness were gone, and my face was shining!"

Gin had a spiritual makeover. God has issued a gift certificate for each and every one of us to experience an ultimate makeover in the spa of His love. All we have to do is accept His invitation. What are we waiting for? Let's get started!

chapter 2

SPIRITUAL MAKEOVER:

Exchanging the Old for the New

Julianna came out of the womb ready to meet every challenge with determination, every celebration with enthusiasm, and every mystery with the passion of discovery. Her fiery red hair was matched only by her fiery personality. She never did anything halfway, but with the throttle full speed ahead. Of the Prices' three children, Julianna was the one who frequented the emergency room for stitches due to throwing caution to the wind as she whirled through her childhood.

One day when Julianna was twelve years old, she was rushing out the front door on her way to dance class. She slammed the door behind her, but the door closed before all of her fingers followed her body across the threshold. You have probably slammed your fingers in the door a time or two and can remember wincing a bit. But Julianna never did anything halfway. She jerked to a sudden halt, spun around, and saw her appendages trapped in the closed door. When she opened the door to remove her hand, she was horrified to discover that not all of it was there. She had amputated the upper third of her second right finger.

"Help! Somebody help me! I've just cut off my finger!"

Fortunately, the woman picking her up for dance class was a nurse. She rushed to the screaming ballerina. "Julianna, where's your mom?" she asked.

"She's not here," Julianna answered between sobs. "Nobody's here but Daniel."

"Quick," the neighbor instructed, "Let's put some pressure on that nub. Daniel, come help us!"

Daniel, Julianna's fifteen-year-old brother, ran down the stairs at the cry for help.

"Julianna's just cut her finger off. You have to find it. We've got to put it in some ice and take her to the hospital right away."

A pale-faced Daniel went to the scene of the accident. As Daniel hung his head, he saw the finger lying at his feet. Trying not to lose his breakfast, Daniel picked up his sister's digit in a towel and handed it over to the nurse.

The good news is that they got to the hospital in time. The skilled doctor put Humpty Dumpty back together again and told them to pray that the finger would reattach.

A few days later Julianna unwrapped the bandages, afraid of what she might find underneath. What she saw was not a pretty picture. Instead of a finger, she saw a black mushroom-like tip.

"Doctor, we took the bandage off today. It's black and crusty and looks like a mushroom cap or a thimble," her mom reported.

"That's fine," he answered. "Don't worry. If nature is working properly, and it sounds like it is, the top will turn black, but underneath, nerves and blood vessels are reattaching. Underneath the thimble, a new finger is forming. She needs the old part in order for the new part to form underneath. In about three weeks, we'll know if the procedure worked. Just keep it wrapped and clean. We'll keep our fingers crossed."

Four weeks after this incident, I received a letter from my little redheaded friend. At the bottom she wrote, "P.S. Guess what? My crusty thimble fell off and I have a new finger!"

Now don't ask me how this happened. It is a mystery to me. But Scripture tells of another mystery that is just as amazing, another grafting process that is just as miraculous. As we have already seen, when God warned Adam and Eve not to eat of the fruit of the Tree of Knowledge of Good and Evil, He warned them that their punishment for disobedience would be death. They did eat, and immediately their spirits died. Their *zoe* life was taken away and they were cut off from God. As a result, every person after that has been born with a dead spirit, including you and me.

But God didn't leave us that way. God demonstrated His love toward us, that while we were still sinners (cut off, dead, rotten to the core), Christ died for us and made it possible for us to be grafted onto the living root—Himself. At the very moment we accept Jesus Christ as our Savior, we receive a new living spirit (*zoe* life) to replace our old dead spirit. He begins our spiritual makeover in the twinkling of an eye by giving us a new birth—in the time it takes for us to say, "I believe." However, the ultimate makeover, God's process of shaping and molding us into the image of Christ, takes a lifetime.

An ultimate makeover, becoming conformed to the image of Christ, begins with a makeover of the spirit. Let's see how He does it.

THE PATH TO LIFE

Makeover articles in magazines always show before-and-after pictures. Usually, the before shots are a bit fuzzy and out of focus, which makes me wonder if the after shot is indeed the same person. Likewise, after we meet Jesus Christ, our change should be so drastic, we should leave friends and family members wondering if we are indeed the same person.

Let's take one last look at what our "before Christ" picture looked like. Just as it is important to know who you are in Christ, it is important to know who you were without Him. Many of these Scriptures that follow may be familiar to you. Don't gloss over them quickly, but read them slowly and carefully, as if you are seeing them for the first time.

- We were dead in our transgressions and sin. (Ephesians 2:1)
- We gratified the cravings of our sinful nature and followed its desires and thoughts. (Ephesians 2:3)
- We were separated from Christ and without hope. (Ephesians 2:12)
- We were far away from God. (Ephesians 2:13)
- We were foreigners and aliens. (Ephesians 2:19)
- We were enemies of God. (Colossians 1:21)
- We were in darkness. (1 Thessalonians 5:4)
- We were once darkness. (Ephesians 5:8)
- We were condemned. (Romans 8:3)
- We were slaves of sin. (Romans 6:17)
- We were blinded to the truth. (John 12:40)
- We were unable to please God. (Romans 8:8)

Not a very pretty picture. Oh, we may look good on the outside; our peeling may look shiny, polished, and desirable, but before we know Christ, we are ugly on the inside and rotten to the core. We can try to cover up the ugliness with modern day fig leaves such as financial success, flashy cars, impeccable makeup, coordinating accessories, or name-brand clothes, but what lies beneath is dark, despicable, and disgusting.

FOREVER NEW

We were born with a dead spirit, but God didn't leave us that way. Before we were even born (Revelation 17:8b) God made an appointment for us to undergo the ultimate makeover. He has a unique beauty regimen designed for each and every one of us—to make us beautiful from head to toe.

Sometimes it is easy to read about Adam and Eve's failure in the Garden and think to ourselves, *How could they disobey like that?* But the reality is that this is not Adam and Eve's story alone. It is our story as well. We make decisions on a daily basis that dishonor God. We disobey, take charge of our own lives, and become lord of our own ring. Then, like Eve, we try to cover up our shame and even attempt to hide from God.

Do you know the first question God asked in the Bible? After Adam and Eve hid from God, He asked, "Where are you?" God knew exactly where they were, what they had done, and what the Enemy had stolen from them. However, He decided to remain in relationship with them and begin the process of restoration, which was completed on the cross of Calvary. He asks the same question of us today, *Where are you?*

I think "but God" are the two most beautiful words in Scripture. "But God demonstrates His own love toward us, in that while we were yet sinners, Christ died for us" (Romans 5:8 NASB). When did we become sinners? The first time we sinned? No, we were born sinners, and that sin is what separated us from God. While we were yet sinners, He became the perfect sacrifice for us, not to cover our ugliness, but to cleanse us and make us new—once and for all.

Salvation Army officer John Allen once said, "I deserved to be damned in hell, but God interfered."[1] God interfered, intervened, and intercepted our death sentence. He sent His Son, who paid the penalty for our sin, and all we have to do to receive the pardon is accept His wonderful gift.

How do we accept this gift certificate for a spiritual makeover? "If you confess with your mouth, 'Jesus is Lord,' and believe in your heart that God raised him from the dead, you will be saved" (Romans 10:9). When you accept Jesus Christ as your own personal Savior, you are freed from the penalty of sin (spiritual death and eternal separation from God), and He gives you a new living spirit. "Salvation is moving from living death to deathless life."[2]

"All this is from God, who reconciled us [joined us back together] to himself through Christ" (2 Corinthians 5:18). Once there was a Christian group who sang a song with the line, "There's a bridge to cross the great divide." However, when they were recording, someone sang, "There's a cross to bridge the great divide." Suddenly, the group realized it had not been an error at all. We were separated from God because of sin, but He sent His Son to die on Calvary's cross to bridge the great divide.

Why did God do this for us? "For God so loved the world that he gave his one and only Son, that whoever believes in him shall not perish but have eternal life" (John 3:16). Remember the three Greek words for life: *bios, psyche,* and *zoe*? Guess which Greek word is translated *life* in John 3:16? *Zoe*—life of the spirit. When you become a Christian, your spirit is reborn and you begin the ultimate makeover at that very moment. "Therefore, if anyone is in Christ, he is a new creation; the old has gone, the new has come!" (2 Corinthians 5:17). We were crucified with Christ and now we live in Him (Galatians 2:20).

What about our glaring needs? "So then as through one transgression there resulted condemnation to all men, even so through one act of righteousness there resulted justification of life to all men" (Romans 5:18 NASB). All were condemned because of Adam's disobedience, but all who accept Christ are freed because of His obedience. At the moment of your salvation, everything you lost when Adam and Eve sinned in the Garden was returned to you in Jesus Christ. Once again you have

1. Significance because of who you are in Christ.
2. Safety and security because of what you have in Christ.
3. Belonging because of where you are in Christ.

Your glaring needs have been fulfilled and transformed into your glowing attributes. Your makeover comes complete with eternal youth (eternal life), a daily cleansing regimen (the Holy Spirit), a new identity (child of God), a new wardrobe (the righteousness of Christ), and much, much more. Why, many of your friends will do a double take to make sure it's really you!

SALVATION PAST, PRESENT, AND FUTURE

Before creation, there was no time. God created time when He made the sun and the moon. "There was evening and there was morning," one day. Then He created man and woman and placed them in the time-space continuum. For God, there is still no time. God sees it all at once. He is the same yesterday, today, and forever. A thousand years are like a day in His sight. He sees the entire span of time, from the beginning to the end, all at one time. But we are time creatures.

When we use the words, "I have been saved," we think time dimensionally. Salvation for us time creatures involves the past, present, and future.

1. In the past, we were saved from the penalty of sin at the

moment of salvation. Theologians call this justification. This is the beginning of our spiritual makeover.

2. In the present, we are being saved from the power of sin as we become conformed to the image of Christ. Theologians call this sanctification, and it is the process of having the ultimate makeover.

3. In the future, we will be saved from the presence of sin. That will happen when we leave this earth and join Christ in heaven for all eternity. Theologians call this glorification. The makeover will be complete!

> How great is the love the Father has lavished on us, that we should be called children of God! And that is what we are! . . . Dear friends, now we are children of God, and what we will be has not yet been made known. But we know that when he appears, we shall be like him, for we shall see him as he is. (1 John 3:1–2)

OUR NEW IDENTITY

There's a game that I've played many times at conferences and retreats as an icebreaker activity. Each person has the name of a famous or an infamous person taped to her back. The women in the room walk around giving each other clues about who they are. "You always put off worrying until tomorrow." "You had so many children you didn't know what to do." "You were the queen of soul." The point of the game is for each woman to figure out her identity.

As I play that game, I am always struck with its similarity to real life. Many times we determine our identity by what others tell us about ourselves. *You are so smart. You are a loser. You are so pretty. You could do anything you set your mind to. You are so ugly. You are so fat.* After a while, those messages determine how we see ourselves, whether true or false. A mature person realizes that just because another person perceives her a certain way doesn't mean that perception is true.

One of the greatest blessings of becoming a Christian and experiencing a spiritual makeover is receiving a new identity. In the Bible, when God touched and changed a person's life, many times He changed the person's name. He said, "You will be called by a new name that the mouth of the LORD will bestow" (Isaiah 62:2b). Abram became Abraham. Sarai became Sarah. Simon became Peter. Saul became Paul. Likewise, when we accept Christ, God gives us a new identity, a new birth certificate, and a new name.

If you want to know your true identity, you need only look in the mirror of God's Word to discover it. It may be different from what you've heard others say about you, but which do you think is more accurate? Who do you think has a better perception of who you are, your Creator or other creatures just like yourself? If you are a Christian today, the following verses describe your new identity.

My Identity in Christ[3]

Matthew 5:13   I am the salt of the earth (collectively with other believers).

Matthew 5:14   I am the light of the world (collectively with other believers).

John 1:12   I am a child of God.

John 15:5   I am part of the true vine, a channel (branch) of Christ's life.

John 15:15   I am Christ's friend.

John 15:16   I am chosen and appointed by Christ to bear His fruit.

Romans 6:18   I am a slave of righteousness.

Romans 6:22	I am enslaved to God.
Romans 8:14–17	I am a joint-heir with Christ, sharing His inheritance with Him.
1 Corinthians 6:17	I am joined to the Lord and am one spirit with Him.
1 Corinthians 6:19	I am a temple of God. His Spirit dwells in me.
1 Corinthians 12:27	I am a member (part) of Christ's body.
2 Corinthians 5:17	I am a new creation.
2 Corinthians 5:18–19	I am reconciled to God and am a minister of reconciliation.
Galatians 3:26–28	I am a son of God and one in Christ with fellow believers.
Galatians 4:6–7	I am an heir of God since I am a son of God.
Ephesians 1:1	I am a saint.
Ephesians 1:3	I am blessed with every spiritual blessing in heavenly places.
Ephesians 1:5	I am adopted into God's family.
Ephesians 1:13–14	I am sealed in Him with the Holy Spirit, who has been given as a pledge of my inheritance.
Ephesians 2:6	I am seated in heaven right now.
Ephesians 2:10	I am God's workmanship, created in Christ to do His work that He planned beforehand that I should do.
Ephesians 2:19	I am a fellow citizen with the rest of God's people in His family.
Ephesians 4:24	I am righteous and holy.
Philippians 3:20	I am a citizen of heaven.
Colossians 1:13	I am delivered from the domain of darkness and transferred to the kingdom of Christ.

Colossians 3:4	I am an expression of the life of Christ because He is my life.
Colossians 3:12	I am chosen of God, holy, and dearly loved.
1 Thessalonians 5:5	I am a son of light and not of darkness.
Hebrews 3:14	I am a partaker of Christ . . . I share in His life.
1 Peter 2:5	I am one of God's living stones and am being built up (in Christ) as a spiritual house.
1 Peter 2:9–10	I am a member of a chosen race, a royal priesthood, a holy nation, a people for God's own possession to proclaim the excellencies of Him.
1 Peter 2:11	I am an alien and stranger to this world in which I temporarily live.
1 Peter 5:8	I am an enemy of the devil.
1 John 3:1–2	I am now a child of God. I will resemble Christ when He returns.
1 John 5:18	I am born of God and the evil one (the devil) cannot touch me.
Revelation 21:9	I am part of the bride of Christ.

That is a lot to put on a name tag, but that is your new identity. Neil Anderson, in his book *Victory over the Darkness*, notes,

> The reason so many Christians are not enjoying the maturity and freedom which is their inheritance in Christ is because they hold wrong self-perceptions. They don't see themselves as they really are in Christ. They don't understand the dramatic change which occurred in them the moment they trusted in Him. They don't see themselves the way God sees them, and to that degree they suffer from a poor self-image. They don't grasp their true identity. They identify themselves with the wrong Adam.[4]

Remember the apple model? The seeds of an apple determine its identity as a Granny Smith, Red Delicious, or Rome. Likewise, your "seed" determines your identity. Your old seed was the same as Adam's (corruptible, disobedient, and enslaved to sin). Your new seed is the same as Christ's (pure, holy, and a slave to righteousness). You are forever new, and your core being has been changed. "For you have been born again, not of perishable seed, but of imperishable, through the living and enduring word of God" (1 Peter 1:23).

Oh, I can hear some of you mumbling now, "Well, I sure don't feel like salt. I don't feel like a saint. I don't feel like part of the bride of Christ." I'd say the predominant word in those statements is *feel*. We must answer the question, Is the above list the truth? Yes, it is the truth, whether we feel like it or not.

If we continue to label ourselves as sinners rather than saints, we are saying our identity is based on our performance and not the finished work of Christ on the cross. I believe we are saints (our new identity) who often sin (our performance, not our identity). If we say we are sinners by identity, then we are saying that our performance is more important than God's redemptive and finished work on the cross. We are basing our identity on our behavior rather than our new birth, our performance rather than our position. I know many people with "good" behavior who are not going to heaven because of their position—they have not accepted Christ and are spiritually dead. I am not saying we never sin. I'm saying that our sin no longer defines who we are. I was a sinner, but I have been saved by grace. Now I'm a saint who sins.

Perhaps you may say, "I feel like a hypocrite saying those verses about myself when I don't really feel like it." Actually, when you do not act like a child of God, you *are* being a hypocrite, because that's who you really are. If you are in a covenant relationship with God and are not acting like His child, you are living a lie.

I saw a bumper sticker recently that said, "God said it. I believe it. It's true." But God said it, it's true whether we believe it or not. I have to ask myself if I am going to walk through life being jerked around and controlled by my emotions, or if I am going to be controlled by what I know is truth. I've often heard that emotions or feelings are like the tail on a dog. I can assure you that if a dog jumps over a fence, the tail will follow. Similarly, if you start walking in the truth, your emotions will follow—eventually. Someone once said, "Faith is acting like God tells the truth." It is one thing to say we believe God tells the truth, but it is quite another to act like it.

There is nothing we can do to make our new identity in Christ more true or less true than it is at the moment of salvation. A sapling planted in the ground does not become more of a tree as it grows. It becomes more mature as its roots grow deeper, it produces a greater display of leaves as it matures, and it provides more shade and stronger branches for a tire swing, homes for the birds, and beauty for others to enjoy. There is nothing you can do to make your identity more true than at the very moment you accept Christ as your Savior, but there is much you can do to make it have more power in your life as you mature. It begins by believing the truth—and the truth will set you free (John 8:32). It is a step of faith. "Faith is being sure of what we hope for and certain of what we do not see" (Hebrews 11:1). It is "acting like God tells the truth."

"But I don't act like a saint," I hear you say. Sometimes I may not act like a saint, but that is my new identity nonetheless. It is not based on performance but position; not how I act, but who I am. When I was five years old, I acted more like a boy than a girl. I climbed trees, shunned dolls, threw rocks, and balked at having to wear a shirt. But I can assure you, that didn't make me a boy—I was a girl.

Let me give you this example. When I was born physically, I had a father. His name was Allan Edwards. As his daughter, I not only had his name, I had his blood coursing through my veins. We were blood related. There was nothing I could do to change that. What if I ran away from home and even changed my name? Would I still be an Edwards? Yes, my name may be different, but I would still be an Edwards.

There is nothing I can do to change my position as Allan Edwards's physical daughter, and once I have accepted Christ, there is nothing I can do to change my position as God's spiritual daughter. My behavior may change the closeness of the relationship with both, but my position as my earthly father's child and my heavenly Father's child stands unchanged.

Do me a favor. Put this book down in your lap. Now clasp your hands together and notice which thumb is on top, your right thumb or left. Open your hands and clasp them together again with the opposite thumb on top. Does that new position feel uncomfortable? Likewise, accepting your new identity in Christ may feel uncomfortable at first, but by spending time with the One who changed you, you'll begin to see yourself as God sees you: absolutely beautiful!

Debbie's Acceptance of Her New Identity

Debbie's paternal grandparents had a housekeeper and groundskeeper who lived in their basement apartment. Silas and Nina were like part of the family and had lived with the grandparents for as long as Debbie could remember. On many occasions, when Debbie's parents and grandparents went out to dinner, she and her younger brother and older sister were left in the care of Silas and Nina. The girls' family had no idea that Silas was molesting their precious children time and time again.

From the time Debbie and Beth were three and six years old until they were ten and thirteen, Silas fondled and sexually molested the girls in the basement apartment lit only by the black and white television blinking in the background while their brother slept in another room. While Silas ravaged Debbie's body, her sister held her face in her hands and told her stories. Together, the girls escaped to a land far away while the worst nightmare imaginable was played out before them.

Silas warned them, "If you tell anybody, I'll hurt your brother." So the girls suffered in silence.

When Debbie was ten years old, she and her sister spent the night with her maternal grandmother while her parents were away on a business trip. The elderly grandmother paused at the opened door to watch her precious granddaughters kneeling beside their bed. With arms wrapped around each other, they began to say their prayers. What began as a tranquil picture of innocence transformed into a nimbus cloud of horrible darkness. Their grandmother clutched her heart as she heard the two little girls pray.

"Dear God, thank You for Mommy and Daddy and Kevin, and Grandma and Grandpa Wilson, and Grandma James. We pray that you will protect us from Silas and keep him from hurting us and touching us in private places. We pray . . ."

The rest was a blur.

The sobbing grandmother rushed to the girls and held them to her breast. A few hours later, in the wee hours of the morning, their parents came back from their business trip, two days early. The girls could hear their parents crying in the next room, but nothing was ever mentioned about Silas. All they knew was that the next time they went to Grandma and Grandpa Wilson's, Silas and Nina were gone.

Years passed with little mention of the years of abuse by Silas. Like old war veterans who never mention the horrors of battle, the girls never mentioned the molestation again. However, the chronic pain of the past was an undercurrent to their total existence. Debbie felt dirty, used, and cheap. She felt like damaged goods.

Debbie accepted Jesus Christ as her Savior when she was a small child, but she had a difficult time believing He could accept her. She didn't see herself as a precious holy child of God dressed in robes of righteousness. She saw herself as a dirty orphan dressed in tattered rags. Then one day, she went to a Bible study and heard for the first time about her identity as a child of God.

"I didn't feel like a holy child of God, but that's who the Bible said I was," she explained. "I read and reread that list of who I am in Christ. The more I studied about my new identity and the truth that sets us free, the more I began to accept it as true. I began to realize it was Satan who held up the picture of Silas and what he had done to me—to remind me of who he wanted me to believe I was. But that was a lie. God took the truth and massaged it into my broken heart like a healing ointment. He placed a princess's crown of beauty on my head and washed away the ashes. He gave me the oil of gladness instead of mourning and dressed me in a garment of praise instead of despair. No longer is my identity determined by what happened to me as a child. My identity is determined by what happened in me through Jesus Christ."

Debbie accepted her new identity that came with her spiritual makeover. It was there all along, like a cloak waiting to be placed on the princess's regal shoulders. She received the robe of righteousness and now walks with the confidence of a dearly loved child of the King. To me, she looks like a queen. Debbie is one of my heroes.

What about you? Have you accepted your new identity? Are you ready to start believing the truth? God's asking, dear one, "Where are you?"

chapter 3

MIRROR, MIRROR ON THE WALL:

Seeing Yourself as God Sees You

Long, long ago, in a land far away, there lived a lovely young princess named Snow White. Her stepmother, the queen, was very cruel and jealous of Snow White's beauty. Every day, the vain queen approached her magic mirror and asked, "Mirror, mirror on the wall, who's the fairest of us all?" For many years, the mirror answered, "You are fairest of all, O Queen." But Snow White grew from a little girl into a fair young maiden, and as the saying goes, the mirror doesn't lie.

One day, the queen approached her magic mirror and asked, "Mirror, mirror on the wall, who's the fairest of us all?" Much to her regret, the queen heard the answer she knew would inevitably come.

"Fair is thy beauty, Majesty, but behold—a lovely maid

I see, one who is more fair than thee. Lips red as a rose, hair black as ebony, skin white as snow . . ."

At once the queen shrieked in anger, knowing that the mirror spoke of none other than Snow White, her beautiful stepdaughter. At once the queen decided to eliminate her competition. She ordered one of her huntsmen to kill the fair princess in yonder woods.

The next day, the huntsman took the princess to the woods, but he could not bring himself to end the life of one so lovely. Thus, he left her in the forest, hoping the queen would think he had accomplished his mission. Meanwhile, Snow White stumbled across seven adorable dwarfs with giant hearts who loved and cared for her.

The next day, the evil queen asked the mirror once again, "Mirror, mirror, on the wall, who's the fairest of us all?"

Once again, the mirror answered, "Snow White."

Realizing her competition was not dead, the queen transformed herself into an ugly old lady (which did not take much effort, I might add) and went to find the girl. When she did, she devised a foolproof plan to offer Snow White a poisoned apple that would cast her into an eternal sleep.

The dwarfs had warned Snow White not to talk to any strangers while they were away doing their chores in the forest. But when the witch came bringing the tempting apple, Snow White took the fruit, ate a bite, and fell into a sleep that was supposed to last forever.

As a child, I remember reading the story of Snow White and almost crying at the fate of one so lovely. As an adult, I read the story and realize it is more than a fairy tale; it is our story as well. Satan was once a lovely prince. Ezekiel describes him as once being "full of wisdom and perfect in beauty" with every precious stone as his covering. He was the anointed cherub who was on the mountain of God (Ezekiel 28:12–14). But pride was his downfall; he wanted to be like God. As a result, God cast Satan from heaven with one-third of all the angels (Isaiah 14:12–23). After his downfall, he was no longer the "fairest of them all."

Satan, like the cruel and wicked queen, then came after us with the poisoned fruit of disobedience.

But the story of Snow White didn't end with her caught in the evil spell. One day a handsome prince came riding through the forest on his white horse. When he saw Snow White deep in sleep, he fell in love with her and placed a kiss upon her lips. When he did, she sat up, blinked her eyes, and sprang to life. The prince scooped Snow White into his arms and took her off to his castle where they lived happily ever after.

Oh dear sisters, a handsome prince has come into our lives as well. His name is Jesus. Our Prince has placed a kiss upon our lips, taken us into His strong arms, and lifted the evil curse. He is the fairest of them all!

We don't need a magic mirror to tell us how fair we are. The Bible is the only mirror we need. When we look into God's Word, He tells us exactly who we are, what we have, and where we are— spiritually beautiful in Christ. Let's take a closer look in the only mirror that matters and examine the reflection we find there.

WHO WE ARE IN CHRIST

We Are Saints (Ephesians 1:1)

When speaking at a women's conference, if I ask everyone who is a sinner saved by grace to raise their hands, most hands in the room shoot up in the air. However, if I ask how many are saints, I see very few hands, if any, go up. Yet Paul never once wrote "to the sinners at Philippi" or "to the sinners at Corinth." He always referred to Christians as saints. He wrote: "To the church of God which is at Corinth, to those who have been sanctified in Christ Jesus, saints by calling, with all who in every place call on the name of our Lord Jesus Christ, their Lord and ours" (1 Corinthians 1:2 NASB).

Paul did refer to himself as the "worst of sinners" (1 Timothy 1:16). But many scholars believe he was referring to his life before he met Jesus on the road to Damascus.

> Paul claims that of all sinners he was "the worst," "first" or "chief." He felt this way because he had persecuted Christ's followers so vigorously. As far as morality was concerned, young Saul had been a strict Pharisee, living a life that was blameless before the law (Phil 3:5-6). Yet in his case as chief sinner, Christ's "unlimited patience" had been displayed as an example to all who would believe in Jesus and thus receive eternal life. Paul's life was a powerful demonstration of what divine grace can do.[1]

That same divine grace is what allows us to be called saints!

The predominant message of the New Testament is that we are all saints by the grace of God, sanctified because we are in Christ—not because we've earned the title, but because Jesus earned it for us. We are not mere sinners who struggle to do better and be better, hanging on until Jesus returns. We have a new identity. No longer are we simply a product of our past failures, hurts, and disappointments, but a result of Jesus Christ's finished work on the cross.

We are saints (by calling) who sometimes sin, but the term "sinners saved by grace" is not recorded in Scripture.[2] Scripture says, "For you have been born again, not of perishable seed, but of imperishable, through the living and enduring word of God" (1 Peter 1:23). As in the apple model, you have a new seed, a new core, a new identity, and a new confidence as a saint. A saint is not a person who is perfect, but one who is set apart.

When did you become a sinner? The first time you sinned? No, you were born a sinner. When did you become a saint? The first time you acted like a saint? No, you became a saint when you were born again.

We Are the Salt of the Earth (Matthew 5:13)

Have you ever tasted potatoes without salt added? They are bland and tasteless. Likewise, a world without Christians would be very unappealing.

Salt has three primary purposes. It preserves, heals, and gives flavor. As Christians, one of our privileges is to preserve what is right and good in the world in which we live. Satan is referred to as a roaring lion (1 Peter 5:8). In our day he prowls around seeking to rip a Christian witness and values from the government, public schools, the entertainment industry, and the very fabric of life. Christians, on the other hand, serve to preserve the values of our godly heritage.

Salt is also an effective healing agent. Gargling with salt water helps heal a sore throat, and swimming in a salty sea helps heal a skinned knee. Likewise, fellowshipping with "salty" Christians helps heal wounded souls by introducing them to spiritual, mental, and physical wellness afforded them through a relationship with *Jehovah Rapha*—the One who heals.

The most common use of salt is to add flavor, and as Christians, we add flavor to our world. A gourmet cook once told me that salt not only gives food a salty flavor, but it also brings out the natural flavor of the food to which it is added. As Christians, we should bring out the best in other people.

We Are the Light of the World (Matthew 5:14)

When Jesus looked out among the multitudes and said to His disciples, "You are the light of the world," I imagine a strand of Christmas lights, each adding to the collective brightness reflecting the Light of Christ. For eighteen years, I worked as a dental hygienist. Fourteen of those years I worked with my husband, Steve, and four to six other Christian women. When I think back on those days, I envision our team as a chandelier of lights, individual yet united to shine the light of Christ to our patients. In the reception room, *Newsweek*, *Southern Living*, and *Better Homes and Gardens* were mixed in with *Focus on the Family*, *Guideposts*, and *Decision* magazines.

Steve and his assistant volleyed ideas about various aspects of the Christian faith back and forth like a tennis ball over a net while they worked on patients. Talk about a captive audience! We prayed with patients, sent them books, and listened to their family problems. Someone once asked, "Aren't you afraid you'll offend someone and lose patients?"

"Someone might leave," I answered. "But a person can get into heaven with a cavity, but they can't get to heaven without knowing Christ."

In our own simple way, we were being light in a very dark world.

Think for a moment about what light does. It drives out darkness. Even the smallest birthday candle in a darkened coliseum will push the darkness aside. Jesus encourages Christians not to hide their light under a bushel, but to put it on a stand to be seen by all. Jesus said He is the light of the world. He has put that same light in you. It is part of your new identity.

Robert Louis Stevenson said, "When a happy man comes into a room, it is as if another candle has been lighted."[3] How much more does a Christian who has something to be truly happy about light up a room!

We Are Chosen (Colossians 3:12)

KC was a beautiful blonde freshman at Georgia State University. She was excited to be at college and looked forward to having a fresh start at life. When rush week came around, she was the first to sign up. This was the week when all the girls desiring to become a member of a sorority went from Greek house to Greek house mingling and hoping to be chosen to become a "sister." After the tiring week of parties, constant smiling, and small talk, the girls waited anxiously until the Friday night party to find out who chose them. KC began getting dressed for the celebration when the phone rang.

"Hello," KC answered cheerfully.

"Hi KC, this is Cassie, the rush coordinator. I'm sorry to tell you this, but looking at the list, no one chose you."

Those words, "No one chose you" rang in KC's ears for years.

After a conference at which I was speaking about our new identity in Christ, KC came up and told me this story. She had never told anyone before, but now she was free from the pain of those words. "For the first time in my life, I can let go of that pain, because I realize I *was* chosen. God chose me. He chose *me*. So what if those girls didn't. God chose me, and that's much more impressive than a sorority pin."

God chose you, precious sister. Like a groom who chooses, pursues, and captures the love of his life, He chose you!

We Are God's Workmanship (Ephesians 2:10)

When my son was in elementary school, he created some works of art that had a striking resemblance to that of the world-renowned artist Picasso. However, Picasso's paintings are worth millions of dollars and my son's are valuable only to me. What makes a work of art valuable? Its value is based on the artist who created it. You, dear friend, are a piece of art created by God Himself. King David described it this way:

> For you created my inmost being; you knit me together in my mother's womb. I praise you because I am fearfully and wonderfully made; your works are wonderful, I know that full well. My frame was not hidden from you when I was made in the secret place. When I was woven together in the depths of the earth, your eyes saw my unformed body. All the days ordained for me were written in your book before one of them came to be. (Psalm 139:13–16)

You are a work of art, a masterpiece, a valuable original, one of a kind, created with the brushstrokes of love, and framed in truth.

We Are Adopted into God's Family (Ephesians 1:5)

My friend Debbie took her thirteen-year-old son to the dermatologist to have a few suspicious moles checked out. The doctor asked her, "Is there anyone on your or your husband's side of the family who has had melanoma or any other types of skin cancer?" No, she couldn't think of any. Then he proceeded to ask a few other questions about their family history.

After the exam, her son, Jason, looked up at her and said, "Mom, when the doctor asked about your family history, it doesn't matter. I'm adopted!"

"You're right, Jason," she said. "I totally forgot you were."

I love this story. See, Debbie went through five years of infertility treatment and two years waiting to adopt a child. Eight months after she adopted Jason, she found out she was pregnant with Jordan. Amazingly, these boys have looked like twins for most of their lives. Just now, as Jason has gone into his growth spurt, can I even tell them apart.

But the sweetest part of the story is Debbie forgot Jason was adopted. Ephesians 1:5 says that we have been adopted as sons through Jesus Christ. God has chosen us to be His own—we're Jesus' adopted brothers and sisters. I think that God, like Debbie, probably forgets we're adopted—He just sees us as His children.

We are saints, the salt of the earth, the light of the world, chosen by God, God's workmanship, and adopted into His family. These are just six of the many verses that describe your new identity in Christ. You are also a child of God, holy, and dearly loved.

WHAT WE HAVE IN CHRIST

We Have Been Blessed with Every Spiritual Blessing (Ephesians 1:3)

"I can't do it! I'm not smart enough, talented enough, and I don't have sufficient training." How God must shudder to hear His children say those words. How many times have those words come out of my mouth! The truth says, "I have been blessed with every spiritual blessing in the heavenly places" (see Ephesians 1:3 NASB). With that on my résumé, "I can do everything through Him who gives me strength" should be the answer to every task God gives me to do.

I'll never forget the day I was sitting in a room full of executives from Moody Press explaining the vision of Proverbs 31 Ministries and our desire to publish books to encourage women in their various roles. Right in the middle of one of my presentations describing a book proposal, one of the directors interrupted me and asked, "Excuse me, Sharon. May I ask, what was your major in college?"

Sheepishly I answered, "I have a bachelor's degree in dental hygiene."

My mind raced back to an earlier time when a television news segment showed Lysa TerKeurst and me taping our international radio program that ministers to women. While explaining the growth and success of the program, the commentator said, "Sharon and Lysa are not trained radio professionals . . ." At first I thought, *He didn't have to say that.* But then I chuckled and agreed. He was right!

No, I do not have a degree in English, creative writing, radio, public speaking, or theology. But I have been blessed with every spiritual blessing in the heavenlies—and so have you!

We Have Been Given the Holy Spirit as a Down Payment (Ephesians 1:14)

The Peter we see in the Gospels and the Peter we see in Acts do not seem like the same man. It is obvious that between the crucifixion of Jesus when Peter denied Jesus three times and Pentecost a few days later when he preached powerfully and led three thousand people to Christ, Peter had a confidence makeover. What exactly happened? He received the gift of the Holy Spirit.

Before Jesus left His disciples, He made them some powerful promises. "The Holy Spirit, whom the Father will send in my name, will teach you all things and will remind you of everything I have said to you" (John 14:26). "But you will receive power when the Holy Spirit comes on you; and you will be my witnesses in Jerusalem, and in all Judea and Samaria, and to the ends of the earth" (Acts 1:8).

Peter did receive that power, and he commenced to change the entire world. The good news is God has given you that same power! Jesus said, "I tell you the truth, anyone who has faith in me will do what I have been doing. He will do even greater things than these, because I am going to the Father" (John 14:12).

God has given you the power of the Holy Spirit—and that's just the down payment of what is to come.

We Are Co-Heirs with Christ (Romans 8:17)

Imagine you have just been informed that you have inherited a multilevel mansion equipped with every conceivable treasure. You run up the curving brick sidewalk, throw open the massive oak doors, and excitedly run from room to room hardly believing the good fortune bequeathed to you! However, what you discover are not the surroundings fit for a queen that you expected, but sensible chambers, adequately furnished and sparsely decorated.

In the foyer, a beautifully carved winding staircase, adorned with plush crimson carpet, beckons you to climb to the next level. You consider the steps, but look back over your shoulder and decide, "Hey, the lower level's enough for me. Besides, I'm afraid of heights. I'll just stay down here where it's safe."

Unbeknownst to you, the upper levels house all the treasures intended to become your inheritance, and you're standing in the servants' quarters. Upstairs await a gilded ballroom, a chandeliered dining hall, four-poster beds with down-filled mattresses, a safe filled with enough gold and silver to last a lifetime, and a jewelry box brimming with family heirlooms.

All that stood between you and these treasures was the staircase. What kept you on ground level? Contentment with mediocrity, lack of knowledge, and a fear of the unknown.

We all have an inheritance from our heavenly Father. We are joint-heirs with Jesus Christ. But oftentimes we spend our days in the servants' quarters, never climbing the stairs to where the true riches are stored.

We can move forward with confidence knowing that whatever He calls us to do, He will provide what we need. He doesn't necessarily call the qualified, but He qualifies the called. We are blessed with every spiritual blessing, joint heirs with Christ, and given the Holy Spirit as a down payment.

WHERE WE ARE IN CHRIST

We Are in Christ (Ephesians 1:4)

One of the most sought-after positions of any junior high school student is to be considered part of the "in crowd." Well, I have good news for you. If you are a Christian, you are in the only "in crowd" that matters. As a child, I often heard the phrase that we can have Jesus in our hearts, but I do not ever remember hearing that we can *be in Him.* Yet, for every one time the Bible says that Christ is *in the believer,* there are ten that say that the believer is *in Christ.* At least forty times in the small book of Ephesians, Paul writes that a Christian is *in Christ.* Take a look at just these verses.

> Praise be to the God and Father of our Lord Jesus Christ, who has blessed us in the heavenly realms with every spiritual blessing *in Christ.* For he chose us *in him* before the creation of the world to be holy and blameless in his sight. In love he predestined us to be adopted as his sons *through Jesus Christ,* in accordance with his plea-sure and will—to the praise of his glorious grace, which he has freely given us *in the One he loves. In him* we have redemption through his blood, the forgiveness of sins, in accordance with the riches of God's grace that he lavished on us with all wisdom and understanding. . . . *In him* we were also chosen, having been pre-destined according to the plan of him who works out everything in conformity with the purpose of his will, in order that we, who

were the first to hope *in Christ*, might be for the praise of his glory. And you also were included *in Christ* when you heard the word of truth, the gospel of your salvation. Having believed, you were marked *in him* with a seal, the promised Holy Spirit. (Ephesians 1:3–13, italics added)

One spring, we hosted a ten-year-old foreign exchange student from Russia. Before he left, he gave us a set of graduated wooden Russian dolls. The first one was about one inch tall and it fit inside a larger one, which fit inside a larger one, which fit inside yet another larger one. What a picture of being in Christ.

Before Jesus went to the Cross, He prayed for you and for me. He said, "On that day, you will realize that I am in my Father, and you are in me, and I am in you" (John 14:20). Jesus in you in Jesus in God.

Anabel Gilham, in her book, *The Confident Woman*, suggests getting three envelopes of graduated sizes and a small slip of paper. On the largest of the envelopes, print GOD. On the next size down, print JESUS. On the smallest of the three, print your name. Then on the slip of paper, print JESUS. Now, put the slip of paper (Jesus) in the smallest envelope (you). Place that envelope into the next smallest envelope (Jesus). Finally, place that envelope into the largest one (God). Now you have a picture of John 14:20. Before anything can get to you, it has to go through God the Father, through Jesus the Son, and when it gets to you, it finds you filled with Jesus. "Look where you are! Secure. Safe. Sheltered. Hidden. Surrounded by love."[4]

We Are Citizens of Heaven (Philippians 3:20)

During our foreign exchange student's stay with us, we had many challenges. His mastery of the English language was very limited, and we were dependent on hand signals and facial expressions to get by. On one occasion, I was trying to get him to write his parents a letter. I pulled out the stationery, handed him a pen, pointed to a picture of his parents, and said, "Why don't we write your parents a letter?" He had no idea what I was talking about.

For twenty minutes, I drew pictures and tried to get him to understand. Finally, with tears in his eyes, he looked up at me and said, "What do?"

I just hugged him and put the pen and paper away.

Sometimes, I feel just like our little Russian guest. I don't understand the cruelty I read in the papers and hear on the news. I am confused at the angry attitudes of drivers with road rage. I don't understand how an adult could harm a child. In confusion I look to my heavenly Father and say, "What do?"

But then God reminds me that I will never feel at home here on earth, because I am an alien, a foreigner. My true citizenship is in heaven, and I'm just a foreign exchange student here for a short while.

Many Christians have known the saving power of Jesus Christ for ten, twenty, or thirty years, but they never understood their true identity as a child of God. They have gone through life feeling inferior, inadequate, and insecure. But when we understand our personage—who we are—that dispels feelings of inferiority. When we understand our possessions—what we have—that dispels feelings of inadequacy. When we understand our position—where we are—that dispels feelings of insecurity. Look in the mirror of God's Word and discover who you really are.

A WRONG PERCEPTION OF THE TRUTH

Once there was a woman named Mildred who was about sixty-five years old. Mildred had spent the entire day at a shopping mall and was leaving with her arms loaded down with packages. Upon exiting the mall, she approached the parking lot and noticed six foreign men sitting in her car. Now, I would have gone and gotten the security guard, but not this spunky lady. She marched right over to the car and yelled, "Get out of my car!"

The six men probably could not understand English, and they simply turned their heads in the opposite direction. What do you do when someone can't speak English? Of course, you say it louder.

"Get out of my car this instant!" Mildred yelled.

Again, they turned their heads, ignoring this little older lady.

Mildred's husband was a retired state patrolman. He had taught her how to use a gun and insisted that she carry one at all times. She calmly put down her packages, pulled out the gun, and tapped one of the men on his shoulder through an opened window.

"Get out of my car!" she yelled once again. They might not have understood English, but the gun they understood. She said she had never seen six men run so fast in all her life.

Satisfied, Mildred picked up her packages, opened the passenger side door, and put her packages on the front seat. Then she slid in behind the wheel, got her key out of her pocketbook, and proceeded to place it in the ignition. Suddenly, she had a sinking feeling in her stomach, as she noticed many things in the car that did not look familiar to her. She tried to insert the key in the ignition, but it would not fit. It was then she realized—this was not her car!

Mildred jumped out of the car and found hers several rows over. She never saw those six men again.

Mildred had the right key, but the problem was she was sitting in the wrong car. She had a wrong perception of the truth.

Every Christian has the key to becoming spiritually beautiful in Christ. "His divine power has given us everything we need for life and godliness through our knowledge of him who called us by

♦ ♦

his own glory and goodness" (2 Peter 1:3). But many are trapped by a wrong perception of the truth. Many are stuck in the parking lot of life, not able to move forward—holding the right key, but wondering why they can't move forward on their journey to becoming conformed to the image of Christ. If you are feeling stagnant in your journey, perhaps you have a wrong perception of the truth. Perhaps you are sitting in the wrong car, looking in the wrong mirror.

God's Word, the only mirror that matters, shows a reflection of who you are, what you have, and where you are in Christ. He is the fairest of them all, and He has chosen you. And remember—mirrors don't lie.

chapter 4

CONFIDENCE MAKEOVER:

Overcoming Inferiority, Insecurity, and Inadequacy

It was a crisp fall weekend in the rolling hills of Ohio. The leaves had just put on their scarlet, auburn, and burnt orange party dresses for the season, and the first frost had dusted the grassy hills like confetti for a grand celebration. Yes, change was in the air.

I was speaking to a group of women for their annual fall retreat. The committee had worked for months preparing the decorations, planning the food, and praying a covering of protection over each potential attendee. The theme for the weekend was "Unveiling the Bride of Christ," and several of the women had displayed their satin, lace, and pearl-studded wedding gowns on mannequins across the stage. A rose arbor at the entrance of the sanctuary gave the illusion that each participant was indeed a beautiful bride as she passed under the arches and down the red-carpeted aisle. A guest registry, complete with quill pen, recorded honored guests as they arrived. The key Bible verse for the weekend was printed on the program.

> But whenever anyone turns to the Lord, the veil is taken away.
> Now the Lord is the Spirit, and where the Spirit of the Lord is,
> there is freedom. And we, who with unveiled faces all reflect the
> Lord's glory, are being transformed into his likeness with ever-
> increasing glory, which comes from the Lord, who is the Spirit.
> (2 Corinthians 3:16–18)

Amanda was among those on the leadership team who were praying for the spiritual veil to be lifted from those attending the conference. Little did she know the veil to be lifted would be her own.

In elementary school, Amanda emerged as a leader among her peers. She was constantly ringed by admiring classmates and praised by adoring teachers as she excelled in every subject. Even as a young child, Amanda showed great promise as a musician, learning to play various instruments with great ease and fluidity.

Amanda moved into junior high school with great confidence in her abilities as a student, talents as a musician, and charisma as a leader. However, unlike in her smaller elementary school, she was not at the top of her class scholastically, nor did she shine socially. She struggled in her schoolwork and in making friends. Her grades went down; her weight went up; and her confidence plummeted.

"I don't know what happened exactly," Amanda said. "I felt as though someone had come in and stolen my confidence. I wasn't doing well in school, which led me to believe I had lost my ability to do so. I remember one of my teachers saying, 'Amanda, your writing is excellent. You express yourself beautifully on paper. But the minute you open your mouth, you're an accident waiting to happen.' From that time on, I never spoke up in class again. I felt stupid, ditzy, and feared I would say something in class to confirm my teacher's estimation of me.

"My sinking self-esteem also affected one of my greatest passions —playing musical instruments. Because I made mistakes and fumbled with the notes, I decided that I had no talent. After a while, I put my flute in its case and stored it in the back of my closet along with many of my hopes and dreams. I had no talent, so why try? I also closed the wooden cover over my piano keys, and the melodious sounds that once filled my parents' home fell silent.

"I was the youngest of four children. During this same period of time, two brothers and one sister left home for college and careers. One brother was a medical doctor in a hospital overseas, one worked for the government in international trade, and my sister was studying concert piano and voice in a major university. Then there was me—a loser."

Amanda told me she felt like a failure at every turn, living in the shadow of her successful siblings. All she wanted to be was a wife and mother. In her parents' eyes that was not enough, and they were disappointed that she had so little ambition or drive to succeed. She also felt they would be glad when she was "out of their hair."

During her junior year in high school, Amanda recalls the sting of a conversation she overheard among her parents and their friends.

"Next year you'll be empty nesters. Can you believe it?" the friend asked.

"Oh, we're kind of looking forward to it," her parents replied.

Actually, during her last two years of high school, they acted as if they already were empty nesters—leaving Amanda at home alone for days while they traveled on business trips around the world.

Dejected and alone, Amanda felt inferior to her brothers and sister, inadequate as a student and a woman, and insecure, with no one who loved her just because of who she was. However, during her first year of college, she met a young man who spoke words of love and promise. When he proposed, she said yes, because she didn't know what else to do with her life. Even though her parents urged the two young people to wait and not drop out of college, Amanda grabbed at her chance of happiness and love before it had a chance to slip away.

Amanda explained, "As I walked down the aisle on my wedding day, the day that should have been the happiest day of my life, I felt like a failure and a disappointment to my family. I entered marriage as a wounded individual with a self-esteem so low, there was no way I could be a 'helper' to someone else."

It wasn't long before Amanda's husband began to make comments that she was stupid and a poor excuse as a wife. She believed him.

After their first year of marriage, Amanda heard the gospel for the first time and immediately accepted Jesus Christ as her Savior. What a balm it was to know there was someone who loved her just the way she was. However, those feelings of inferiority, insecurity, and inadequacy (the three-headed monster) still ruled her life and her emotions. She had very little confidence as a wife, a mother, or a child of God.

During the weekend retreat, God opened Amanda's eyes to the truth of Scripture. She saw that she was a dearly loved child of God who has been blessed with every spiritual blessing in the heavenly places. She saw for the first time that it was Satan's lies that kept her in bondage to feelings of worthlessness. It was the Enemy who told her she was stupid, unlovely, unworthy, and a failure. But that was not the truth at all. It was a lie.

"I learned that the Bible says I am chosen, I am holy, I am dearly loved, I have the mind of Christ, and I can do all things through Christ who gives me strength. I may not have my Ph.D., I may not have a college degree, but my name is written in the Lamb's Book of Life, and that's the only credential I need."

Also, at the retreat, I encouraged the women to go back to the Enemy's camp and take back what he had stolen from them. In 1 Samuel, King David's enemies attacked his men and stole their wives and children. King David did not accept defeat. Rather he and his men prepared for battle, marched into the enemy's camp, and took back what the enemy had stolen. Likewise, we have an enemy who has stolen from us. John 10:10 describes Satan as an enemy who comes to steal, kill, and destroy. He steals our peace, he steals our joy, and he steals our dreams. Like King David and his mighty men, we need to go to the Enemy's camp and take back what he has stolen from us.

After the retreat, Amanda decided to go home and do just that.

The next day, she opened her closet, reached back through the clutter, and pulled out her flute, which had laid dormant for several years. With newfound confidence in Christ, she placed it to her lips, closed her eyes, and began playing as she had never played before. Heavenly music filled her home and her heart. God restored her confidence, her ability, and her talent, which the Enemy's lies had stolen many years before. Amanda then uncovered the piano keys and her nimble fingers played as if she were a practiced musician. Notes that had long been silent sprang to life at her fingertips.

Amanda's transformation was phenomenal. I must tell you that she is one of the most beautiful women I have ever met. No one would have guessed that she felt unconfident, unattractive, unlovable, unintelligent, untalented, and unworthy. But when Amanda found out who she is in Christ, what she has in Christ, and where she is in Christ, she experienced a confidence makeover and became beautiful from the inside out. She truly glows with the radiance of Christ. Now when Amanda hears destructive criticism aimed at belittling her abilities or devaluing her as a person, she reminds herself, "God says that I am chosen, dearly loved, clothed with righteousness, and equipped with the mind of Christ! And He always tells the truth."

Amanda had a confidence makeover. You can have one too!

THE BARBIE SYNDROME

Psychologist Dr. James Dobson notes that lack of self-esteem is one of the greatest problems among women today, and it's easy to see why. It's not easy being a girl. We are expected to be Betty Crocker in the kitchen, Mother Teresa in the community, Jane Fonda in the gym, Mary Kay Ash in the boardroom, and Marilyn Monroe in the bedroom—all while looking fit, fresh, and firm. The media spend so much time trying to define women's roles that we've lost God's perspective on one of His most amazing creations— woman. In this beauty- and youth-oriented culture, she's expected to remain beautiful, slender, and active her entire life. These expectations are causing women everywhere to feel like they don't measure up, they can't quite cut it, and they aren't the women that society expects them to be. As the media have attempted to push the modern woman in these directions, she has found herself more unfulfilled, less content, lonelier, and less confident than ever before. In the seventies, Helen Reddy sang, "I am woman hear me roar in numbers too big to ignore." But the woman of the new millennium is more likely to be heard singing, "I am woman. I am invincible. I am tired."

Before teaching a seminar on the unrealistic expectations placed on women today, I decided to find a visual icon to make a lasting impression on my audience, so I visited the local toy store.

My desire was to buy a Barbie. I have a teenage son, and I had not walked down those pink aisles in the toy store in quite some time. I was surprised to discover that you don't simply go to a toy store and buy *a* Barbie. There are hundreds of different types of Barbies. I was amazed to discover all this little lady had accomplished in the past twenty-five years or so since I had seen her last. I had known Barbie when she was simply a regular doll with a nice figure, some smashing party clothes, a handsome boyfriend named Ken, and an orange convertible with teal interior. But she's come a long way, and here are just a few of her accomplishments. She's now a dentist, a surgeon, a veterinarian, a cheerleader, an animal rights activist, a professional basketball player for the WNBA, a child-care worker, a store clerk, an Olympic gymnast, an aerobics instructor, a race car driver, and a soldier—just to name a few. She even has her own Web page (which of course anybody who's anybody must have). Alas, in the year 2000 we received the news that Barbie was running for political office with the debut of President Barbie. I feel like an underachiever just thinking about it.

Not only has she managed to accomplish formidable achievements; she has remained glamorous, gorgeous, and sexy at the same time. If you blew Barbie up to human size, her measurements would be 38-18-34. Maybe I don't travel in the right circles, but I don't know many women who fit that description. The only blemish I could find on Barbie was "made in Japan" stamped on the bottom of her otherwise perfect foot. No wonder little girls grow up feeling inferior, insecure, and inadequate.

The pressure to do it all and look glamorous while doing it doesn't end in the pink aisle of the toy store. This message is also splashed on high-rise billboards, plastered on slick magazines, aired on nightly television, enlarged on the silver screen, and promoted on the elementary school playground.

In the early eighties, I went to hear a speaker talk about how to be the "total woman." She had some very interesting ideas, especially some creative uses for Saran Wrap. However, as I looked around at the women in the room, there were more who looked like the "totaled woman" than the "total woman." Someone reading this might say, "Well, those girls just need to get into church!" But the problem was, we were in church. Most of the women knew Jesus as Savior, but the peace, joy, and contentment He offers were a distant dream instead of a daily reality.

Instead of being "oaks of righteousness, a planting of the LORD" as Isaiah 61:3 describes, we looked more like Charlie Brown's Christmas tree—sparse, limp, and bent over trying to bear the weight of a single ornament. Oh sure, we can decorate the tree and make it beautiful on the outside, just as Sally, Linus, Snoopy, and Pig Pen decorated Charlie Brown's little tree. But we know what lies underneath the glitter, tinsel, and twinkling lights. As one author said, "Oftentimes under silken apparel, there is a threadbare soul."[1]

Perhaps the second most popular women's magazine topic next to beauty makeovers is having a confidence makeover. You can't walk through the grocery store checkout line without being reminded how insecure women feel today. Magazine racks overflow and bookstore shelves bulge with authors telling us how to boost our confidence and become more assertive, positive, and secure individuals. For example, *Self* magazine featured an article titled "Shortcuts to Confidence: Small Skills, Big Rewards."[2] Let me save you the trouble of reading this article. Basically, the writer said in order to feel confident, fix something. That's right—fix something. She had a lazy Susan. It was broken. She got a Phillips head screwdriver. Fixed it. And she felt triumphant, competent, and empowered. I don't know about you, but it's going to take more than repairing a lazy Susan to make me feel confident.

Covers of magazines are revealing. *Good Housekeeping* featured an article on the "Goldie Rules"—words of wisdom for women on how to be confident, loving, and lovable, according to Goldie Hawn. *Woman's Day* included an article called "Boost Your Confidence: 15 Ways to Feel Great." *YM* magazine for young teens featured an article titled "Confidence Makeovers: 15 Ways to Feel Fab About Youself."

Perhaps my favorite article came from *Salon Ovations Magazine*, called "Super Confidence and How to Get It."[3] The author encouraged readers to never use the word *fail*. "Super confident people simply don't think about failure—they don't even use the word." They use the words "glitch, bungle, or setback instead." Super confident people privately praise themselves for a job well done. They speak firmly and clearly and look the boss in the eye when they mention the five thousand dollar raise. (Are you taking notes? I hope not!) She then tells us to make a tape of "I am" statements and play them in the morning when we get up, in the car on the way to work, on our way home from work, and before we go to bed in the evening. The tape is to contain statements such as "I am glad to be me," "I am confident," and "I am creating the perfect relationship."

These ideas are like the "cheap nails" I mentioned in chapter 1. If we choose to use these types of ideas to build our self-confidence, we will probably fall apart when the strong winds of adversity blow our way. Ninon de L'Enclos said, "That which is striking and beautiful is not always good; but that which is good is always beautiful."

THE THREE-HEADED MONSTER

Three areas that block women from being all that God intends for them to be and from accomplishing all that God intends for them to accomplish include feelings of inferiority, insecurity, and inadequacy. I hear women make comments such as, *I can't do that. I wish I were talented like Sarah. If people really knew me, they wouldn't like me. I'm not very smart. I feel like a failure. I can't do anything right. I could never stand up in front of anyone and speak. I believe the Bible works for her, but I don't believe it would work for me. I don't fit in anywhere. Nobody loves me.*

Where do these feelings come from? From the time we are born, we receive messages about ourselves that are programmed into our minds. We may not realize our minds are being programmed, but it has happened as sure as I'm typing these words on my computer. Either we have been esteemed, encouraged, and embraced or we have been unloved, discouraged, and devalued. These messages have been given both intentionally and unintentionally from family, friends, teachers, and other significant people who have made up our own little world. Early messages were programmed into our minds and formed a type of filter or grid system. Every thought we have, every piece of information we receive must pass through that filter.

For example, little Mari was told at an early age that she was stupid, unattractive, and clumsy. Her ears looked like wings; her teeth looked like a twenty-car pileup; and her legs looked like a flamingo's. In the fourth grade, she got coke bottle glasses and kids called her "four-eyes" on the playground when the teachers weren't close enough to hear. One day in geography class, the room erupted with laughter when she answered that Philadelphia was our nation's capital.

Seven years later, as a high school junior, Mari's head has grown to catch up with her ears, the orthodontist has done a stellar job with her now perfectly aligned white teeth, and her blue contact lenses accentuate the aquamarine hue of her eyes. She was inducted into the National Honor Society and scored 1520 on her SAT. And yet, when Mari walks into a room full of people, she feels like that awkward fourth grader with the big ears, skinny legs, and thick glasses who was laughed at in geography class. Even though she is a beautiful, intelligent young lady, that negative self-destructive filter is still in place, and deception is the glue that holds it there. She does not see herself for who she really is.

Now let's pretend that Mari went to a church retreat and heard the good news of Jesus Christ for the first time. Let's say she made a profession of faith, accepted Jesus as her Savior, and began the journey of making Him Lord over every aspect of her life. What happens to the negative filter that is cemented over her mind? Does it immediately fall off when she becomes a Christian? No, it does not. She probably doesn't even know it is there. Even though Mari is a beloved child of God who has been blessed with every spiritual blessing in the heavenlies, unless she has that negative filter removed by renewing her mind, she will most likely continue feeling inferior, insecure, and inadequate. Only now she may add guilt on top of it for not feeling more like a victorious Christian.

When Mari became a Christian, she received a spiritual makeover. She just didn't know it. It reminds me of a story I heard about two boys arguing if a chicken running around the barnyard with his head cut off was dead or alive. While they were watching this strange phenomenon, a wise old farmer walked up.

"Sir," the boys asked, "is that chicken running around with his head chopped off dead or alive?"

The old farmer scratched his chin and pondered the situation. Finally he spoke, "Well, best I figure, that chicken is dead, but he just don't know it yet."

That pretty much describes many Christians. It described me for about fifteen years of my life after I had become a born-again Christian. My old self was dead, but I just didn't know it yet. I had the spirit of Jesus Christ living in and through me; I just didn't uderstand it yet. I was a saint, the salt of the earth, holy, and dearly loved; I just didn't believe it yet.

A New Identity

Paul said, "Therefore, if anyone is in Christ, he is a new creation; the old has gone, the new has come!" (2 Corinthians 5:17). At the moment of salvation, our *zoe* life is restored and our dead spirit springs to life in Christ. Now we need to change the way we see ourselves as children of God. We need a confidence makeover.

Scripture says, "Forget the former things; do not dwell on the past. See, I am doing a new thing! Now it springs up; do you not perceive it? I am making a way in the desert and streams in the wasteland" (Isaiah 43:18–19).

When we become Christians, every one of those verses describing our new identity in chapter 2 is true. So how do we start acting like we believe the truth? How do we transform our minds to change those feelings of inferiority, insecurity, and inadequacy into feelings of confidence, believing we can do all things through Christ who gives us strength? How do we remove the negative filter and replace it with the truth? We use a powerful deception remover—the Word of God.

John 8:31–32 holds the key to unlocking the prison doors that hold many captive to feelings of inferiority, insecurity, and inadequacy. "If you continue in My word, then you are truly disciples of Mine; and you will know the truth, and the truth will make you free" (NASB). Experiencing a confidence makeover begins by abiding in God's Word. This does not mean simply reading the Bible for information, as a textbook. There have been Bible scholars who have read the Bible for years but do not have a personal relationship with Jesus Christ, nor have they experienced the regenerative, restorative power of the Holy Sprit. "Abide" means to continue in, to remain in, to dwell in, to stand in, to tarry on, to pursue in order to experience.[4] When we abide in God's Word, the negative filter will be removed piece by piece, thread by thread, and our minds will be changed. In order to experience a confidence makeover, we must change the way we think about our personage, our possessions, and our position.

Remember that article in the *Salon Ovations* magazine about making a tape of "I am" statements and playing them when you get up in the morning, on your way to work, on your way home from work, and before you go to bed at night? The "I am" statements were a bit silly, but the method has some merit. Repetition is an excellent way to renew your mind.

I suggest making a list of your new identity in Christ and reading it often. Your bathroom mirror, refrigerator door, and car dashboard would work just fine as places to post your list.

Psychologists agree that we tend to act according to how we see ourselves. If you see yourself as a failure, you will most likely go through life expecting yourself to fail. If you see yourself as a sinner, you will go through life expecting to continue to sin because that's just who you are. If you see yourself as a saint, chosen by God and dearly loved, you will tend to walk in confidence. "No one can consistently behave in a way that is inconsistent with how he perceives himself."[5]

One night a little boy ran up the stairs and crawled into bed. After a few minutes, his mother heard a loud thump on the floor. She ran up the stairs and burst into her son's room. Seeing him in a heap on the floor she asked, "Son, what happened?"

"I don't know," he replied, "I guess I stayed too close to where I got in."

I fear that many have "stayed too close to where they got in." Many have walked the aisle at a church service, signed a commitment card at a revival, or accepted Christ in the quiet of their own home, but then never matured spiritually. They live as though they are the same insecure person they were before they were born again and received the power of the Holy Spirit.

Paul tells us, "We are God's workmanship, created in Christ Jesus to do good works, which God prepared in advance for us to do" (Ephesians 2:10). But many of don't have the confidence to do what God has planned for us to do. Mephibosheth in 2 Samuel 9 was the grandchild of King Saul and the child of Prince Jonathan, but lived like a pauper. When he was a boy, his nurse dropped him while fleeing from their enemies. As a result, he was crippled in both feet.

When David took over the rule of Israel, he wanted to know if there was anyone in Jonathan's household to whom he could show kindness. Jonathan had been David's best friend and he loved him as a brother. A servant told David about the crippled Mephibosheth, and he was summoned immediately. Mephibosheth lived in a place called Lo Debar (meaning a pastureless land).

My own (very unofficial) translation of Lo Debar is "below the bar." Mephibosheth was living below the bar. He was the grandchild of a king, but he was living in a pastureless land like a pauper. When he came before King David he said, "What is your servant, that you should notice a dead dog like me?" (v. 8).

David didn't even answer him. He simply turned to his servant and commanded that all the land that had been Saul's be given back to his grandson and that Mephibosheth should eat at the king's table every day.

Perhaps you are walking around crippled because of something that has happened to you as a child. Perhaps you feel like a "dog." And yet, God is looking to bless you, to restore what has been taken away, and to invite you to feast at His table every day. Mephibosheth was a grandchild of King Saul and potential heir to the throne. However, he saw himself as nothing more than a "dead dog," unworthy to receive even the smallest show of kindness from David. David's desire was to restore to Mephibosheth all the land that would have been his inheritance and invite him to feast at his table daily.

"A dead dog?" I think not.

The Three-Headed Monster Rears His Ugly Head

The three-headed monster of inferiority, insecurity, and inadequacy can paralyze a Christian into inactivity. God's desire is to destroy this monster with the truth and render him impotent in your life. Satan's desire is to feed him with lies and make him control your life. Whom are we going to believe?

Believing who we are in Christ destroys feelings of inferiority. Believing where we are in Christ destroys feelings of insecurity. Believing what we have in Christ destroys feelings of inadequacy. What a transformation when a Christian believes the truth. She experiences a confidence makeover!

I do not want you to think I am always victorious and never struggle with the three-headed monster. He still rears his ugly head every now and then. Let me give you one example.

It was my first large speaking engagement, to about 450 women. My topic was "Unshakable Confidence in Christ." Two weeks before I was to speak to the group, I attended a luncheon. At my table were seated two ladies I did not know, and they were talking about a speaker they had recently heard at the church where I would be speaking in a few weeks.

"He was the most powerful speaker I have ever heard," one said.

"I cried all the way through his testimony. Just to think, he had to live with the fact that his son was an arsonist. Oh how God has worked mightily in the family. The pastor was so moved, he asked him to speak at the Sunday night service—that is highly unusual. I don't think we will ever have a speaker as good as he was again."

On and on they sang the praises of this mighty man of God. They used words like *dynamic, powerful, electric,* and *eloquent.* I never mentioned that I was the speaker for their next meeting. At that point, I wasn't so sure I would be.

As I listened to the ladies, my throat constricted, the tea sandwiches clung to the roof of my mouth, and my heart began pounding wildly. Then Satan, the gatekeeper for the three-headed monster, let him out.

"Who do you think you are, going to speak at this event? Listen to the caliber of people they bring in. This man came from all the way across the country. You are just from across town. What could you possibly have to say to help these women? If I were you, I'd bow out now before you embarrass yourself."

You know what? Even though I knew it was the Enemy whispering in my ear, I started to believe him. After all, what he was saying made a lot more sense than the "I am" statements taped on my refrigerator door.

After the luncheon, I decided to go by the church and purchase a tape of the previous speaker, just to see what I was going to be compared to. I walked into the church, paid my five dollars, popped the tape in the console, and braced myself for the hour of power.

Nothing happened.

I fast-forwarded the tape.

Nothing happened.

I flipped the tape over.

Nothing happened. The tape was blank.

At that moment, I did not hear the dynamic speaker on the tape, I heard God.

Sharon, you do not need to hear what My servant said to these people two weeks ago. The tape is blank because I do not want you to compare yourself to anyone else. It doesn't matter what he said. I will give you a message for these ladies. I can speak through a prophet, I can speak through a fisherman, and I can speak through a donkey.

I gave him a message, and I have given you one as well. Who are you "performing" for, My child, them or Me? Do not compare yourself to anyone. You are My child, and I am asking you to speak for Me alone.

It was indeed an hour of power. I didn't bother getting my money back for the defective tape. It was exactly what I needed to hear.

So the next time Satan said to me, "Who do you think you are?" let me tell you what I said: "I am a child of God. I am part of the bride of Christ. I am a joint heir with Christ. I have the power of the Holy Spirit. I have been delivered from the domain of darkness and transferred to the kingdom of Christ. I am chosen of God, holy, and dearly loved."

Two weeks later I spoke with confidence, and God blessed us all.

Slaying the three-headed monster of inferiority, insecurity, and inadequacy is no easy task. It all begins with understanding the truth of who you are in Christ, what you have in Christ, and where you are in Christ. Is this hard for you to believe? Well, perhaps you need a *faith lift*. Keep reading.

chapter 5

FAITH-LIFT:

Taking God at His Word

CHILDLIKE FAITH

She was among an eager group of four-year-old children crowded around my feet as I taught their Sunday school lesson. I was the teacher and they were the students—or at least that's how it started out. The pint-sized audience listened intently as I tried to create a mental image of Jesus and His disciples trapped in a thunderstorm on the Sea of Galilee.

"The winds bleeeeeew and rocked the little boat back and forth, back and forth. The waves were soooooo big; they splashed over the wooden sides and got the men all wet. Then water started filling up the boat—and do you know what happens when a boat gets full of water?"

"It sinks," they chimed together.

"That's right." I continued with a wrinkled brow and a concerned look on my face. "That's not all. The lightning was sooooo bright, it looked like fire in the sky. And the claps of thunder were sooooo loud, they could feel them vibrate in their chests."

After painting this picture of impending doom and thinking I would have my "congregation" just a little worried about the fate of these men trapped in a storm, I asked the question. "Now if *you* were in a tiny boat like this, caught in a terrible storm like this, would *you* be afraid?"

Then one precious little girl, confident and unshaken by the entire scenario, shrugged her shoulders and replied, "Not if Jesus was in the boat with me."

I will never forget that answer. As her words have echoed in my mind, I've come to realize that this is the answer that should calm all our worries and fears. Just as the disciples had the storm raging all around them, many times the storms of life rage around us. A friend discovers she has cancer, a husband loses his job, a child is born with birth defects. These are storms with waves of emotions so high that our lifeboat fills with tears and it appears it could sink at any moment. Waves of fear rock our boat and threaten to spill us into the depths of despair without even a life jacket to keep us afloat. Storms cause us to doubt who we are, what we have, and where we are as a child of God. Waves of emotions rock our faith.

"Tell me, would you be afraid?"

"Not if Jesus was in the boat with me."

And guess what. He is. Although the pain may be great, I don't need to be afraid that the storms of life will destroy me, because He's in the boat with me. That gives me great peace.

After the children filed out and were off to Sunday lunches throughout the city, I sat in the room to digest the words of the real teacher that day. It was childlike faith in its purest form. The little girl believed God.

WORRY LINES

As I get older, I've noticed little lines around my eyes. Some people call them worry lines or crow's feet. I prefer to call them laugh lines. I was not surprised to read that the most common form of plastic surgery performed in this country is the face-lift. Likewise, to keep us beautiful on the inside, I think many of us need a faith-lift. We need to believe God—pure and simple.

After Adam and Eve disobeyed God and ate the forbidden fruit in the garden, the bottom-line emotion they experienced was fear. They hid from God and feared His presence. I believe a bottom-line emotion for us today is still fear. We fear rejection, financial ruin, unemployment, losing a child, losing a husband, illness, getting old and dying—just to name a few.

One day I watched a program on *Oprah* on which women discussed their fear of aging and "losing their looks." One woman, with tears in her eyes and a quivering lip, told her fear of aging and not "being beautiful" any longer. She was thirty years old. If she is worried about losing her beauty at thirty, I can only imagine the worry lines she'll have by the time she's fifty.

Fear of the future riddled with "what-if's" and regret of the past riddled with "if only's"—these are two paralyzing emotions that can only be erased by faith in God's character and His truth.

WHAT IS FAITH?

Hebrews 11:1 gives us a wonderful definition of faith: "Now faith is being sure of what we hope for and certain of what we do not see." "It is that trust in God that enables believers to press on steadfastly whatever the future holds for them. They know they can rely on God."[1]

Another Bible translation notes, "Now faith is the assurance (the confirmation, the title deed) of things [we] hope for, being the proof of things [we] do not see and the conviction of their reality [faith perceiving as real fact what is not revealed to the senses]" (AMP). I love the idea of a "title deed." That means when Satan comes snooping around and accusing us of being anything less than what God has declared, we need to show him the title deed, the Word of God, to prove him a liar. He will try to move in on conquered territory, but we hold the title deed, and we've been bought with a price and stamped with the official seal—the Holy Spirit.

Another aspect of faith is that it connects the visible and the invisible. In 2 Kings 6, when Elisha's servant woke up one morning terrified because they were surrounded by a host of the enemies on horseback, Elisha asked God to reveal the invisible.

"Oh, my lord, what shall we do?" the servant asked.

"Don't be afraid," the prophet answered. "Those who are with us are more than those who are with them."

And Elisha prayed, "O LORD, open his eyes so he may see." Then the LORD opened the servant's eyes, and he looked and saw the hills full of horses and chariots of fire all around Elisha. (2 Kings 6:15–17)

The Lord may never give us the opportunity of having that veil that separates the visible from the invisible lifted in the physical sense, but I pray the veil of our hearts will be torn from top to bottom, just as the veil in the temple was torn the moment Jesus died on the cross. "So we fix our eyes not on what is seen, but on what is unseen. For what is seen is temporary, but what is unseen is eternal" (2 Corinthians 4:18). The unseen is the greater reality.

Faith is not based on ignorance, but rather on what we know

about the Provider. It means believing God, even though our eyes and emotions tell us differently.

We will never have all of our questions answered this side of heaven, but if we simply strengthen our faith by believing and acting on what little we do know, we'll be mountain moving, giant slaying, women of beauty and strength.

Faith in Who God Is

One crucial aspect to having unshakable confidence in God is basing our faith on *who* God is and not *what* He does. If we base our faith purely on what we see God do with our physical eyes, our journey will be a spiritual roller coaster of ups and downs, twists and turns. We cannot understand the mind of God or His ways. His ways are higher than our ways, and faith is believing that "Father knows best" no matter what.

Three boys who believed God based on who He was regardless of what might happen were Shadrach, Meshach, and Abednego. They were Jewish administrators who served during the time of King Nebuchadnezzar. When they refused to worship the king's idols, but chose to honor the One True God instead, the king threatened to throw them in a blazing furnace. They replied:

> O Nebuchadnezzar, we do not need to defend ourselves before you in this matter. If we are thrown into the blazing furnace, the God we serve is able to save us from it, and he will rescue us from your hand, O king. But even if he does not, we want you to know, O king, that we will not serve your gods or worship the image of gold you have set up. (Daniel 3:16–18)

The boys knew God could rescue them, but if He chose not to, they understood He had a higher reason beyond what they could see.

By the way, do you remember the end of the story? The king tied up the boys with ropes and threw them in the furnace. Then he and his men watched Shadrach, Meshach, and Abednego walk around in the fire with a fourth man who looked like a "son of the gods." Jesus showed up. The king shut up. And the boys were released without even a hint of the scent of smoke. Not only is Jesus in the boat with us, He's in the fire with us as well.

The Object of Our Faith

One day I was talking to my ministry partner, Lysa, on the phone. Her four-year-old daughter, Hope, who was supposed to be taking a nap, came walking into the room her mother was in.

"What are you doing out of bed, young lady?" Lysa asked.

"I'm having my quiet time," she responded matter-of-factly.

Hope plopped down on the couch with her "Bible"—the Sears catalog.

Unfortunately, many view God as someone up in heaven who doles out the goodies and a quiet time as a time to place an order. But He is so much more.

A. W. Tozer wrote, "Nothing twists and deforms the soul more than a low or unworthy conception of God."[2] Our concept of God, our understanding of who He is and what He does, is of crucial importance. Inaccurate and unbiblical thoughts about God can block His power in our lives.

In the Old Testament, there are many names of God that describe His character: He is *Elohim*—the Creator, *El Elyon*—God Most High, *El Roi*—the God who sees, *El Shaddai*—the All-Sufficient One, *Adonai*—the Lord, *Jehovah*—the Self-Existent One, *Jehovah-Jireh*—the Lord will Provide, *Jehovah-Rapha*—the Lord that Heals. When someone in the Old Testament had an encounter with God and learned something new about His character, the person often gave God a new name. Likewise, when we experience a relationship with Him, we will learn new and exciting aspects of His character. However, our perception of God should never be based on our experiences alone. God has given us the Bible to reveal His nature. Through that revelation, God releases His power in our lives—power that enables us to think radically different thoughts that in turn affect our actions and emotions.

Of all the names of God mentioned in the Bible, the one that is the most powerful is I AM. Moses asked God, "Suppose I go to the Israelites and say to them, 'The God of your fathers has sent me to you,' and they ask me, 'What is his name?' Then what shall I tell them?"

God answered, "I AM WHO I AM. This is what you are to say to the Israelites: I AM has sent me to you" (Exodus 3:13–14). That name is so powerful that when Jesus answered the questioning Roman soldiers who were coming to arrest Him with the same answer, they fell over! (John 18:5). Whatever you need, dear friend, God is.

Oswald Chambers once said, "We act like pagans in a crisis—only one out of an entire crowd is daring enough to invest faith in the character of God."3 Yet we can trust Him!

He is unparalleled and unprecedented.
He is the centerpiece of civilization.
He is the superlative of all excellence.
He is the sum of human greatness.
He is the source of divine grace.
His name is the only one able to save,
And His blood is the only power able to cleanse.
His ear is open to the sinner's call.
His hand is quick to lift the fallen soul.

He's the eternal lover of us all—every one,
And you can trust Him.

He supplies mercy for the struggling soul.
He sustains the tempted and the tried.
He sympathizes with the wounded and broken.
He strengthens the weak and the weary.
He guards and He guides the wanderer.
He heals the sick and cleanses the leper.
He delivers the captive and defends the helpless,
And He binds up the broken-hearted.
He's for you . . . and you can trust Him.

Jesus is the key to all knowledge.
He's the wellspring of wisdom.
He's the doorway of deliverance and He's the pathway of peace.
He's the roadway of righteousness.
He's the highway of holiness.
He's the gateway to glory,
And yes—you can trust Him.

Jesus IS enough . . . He's the all sufficient KING . . .
He's the King of the Jews.
He's the King of Israel.
He's the King of Righteousness
And He's the King of the Ages.
He's the King of Heaven.
He's the King of Glory.
He's the King of kings and
He's the Lord of lords.
And "yes" again, you can trust Him.

And rejoice in this my friend . . . He is a Sovereign King.
There is no gauge to measure His limitless love.
There is no barrier to block His blessings outpoured.
He is enduringly strong
And He is entirely supreme.
He is eternally steadfast.
He is immortally faithful.
He is imperially powerful and
He is impartially merciful.
He is Jesus—God's Son—and you can trust Him!

I wish I could more accurately describe Him to you, but
He's indescribable.
He's incomprehensible.
He's invincible.
He's irresistible.

You can't outlive Him, and you can't live without Him.
The Pharisees couldn't stand Him,
But they found they couldn't stop Him;
Pilate couldn't fault Him.
Herod couldn't kill Him.
Death couldn't conquer Him,
And the grave couldn't hold Him!

My friends . . .
He's the Alpha and Omega, the first and the last.
He's the God of the future and the God of the past.
And we rise to speak His Name again and again . . . Jesus . . .
    Jesus.
He is Jesus . . . He is for us . . . and WE CAN TRUST HIM![4]

INCREASING YOUR FAITH

I remember sitting in embryology and anatomy classes in college and being amazed at the intricacies of the human body. It still boggles my mind to imagine that a microscopic strand called DNA determines every part of our physical bodies. It is also a wonder that every muscle we will ever have is present when we are born. Every little trapezius, triceps, biceps, quadriceps, and gluteus maximus—from the top of your head to the tip of your toes—is present and accounted for when you breathe your first breath. That means that you and Arnold Schwarzenegger came with the same basic muscular equipment, but because of exercise, his muscles grew bigger!

Just as a newborn baby has all the muscles she will ever have, as a new *born-again* believer, you received all the faith you will ever need. We are each given a measure of faith (Romans 12:3). However, some have a larger faith (not necessarily more) because they have exercised, stretched, and strengthened what they were given. When the disciples failed to cast out a demon and asked Jesus the reason, He answered, "Because you have so little faith" (Matthew 17:20). It was not the quantity of their faith but the quality—their faith needed more exercise.[5] Jesus went on to say, "I tell you the truth, if you have faith as small as a mustard seed, you can say to this mountain, 'Move from here to there' and it will move. Nothing will be impossible for you."

All I'm talking about in *Ultimate Makeover* is having faith to believe God when He says, "Therefore, if anyone is in Christ, he is a new creation; the old has gone, the new has come!" (2 Corinthians 5:17) and "His divine power has given us everything we need for life and godliness through our knowledge of him who called us by his own glory and goodness" (2 Peter 1:3). For some of you, it may be easier to consider moving a mountain. For some of you, the mountain you need to move is your unbelief.

Hebrews chapter 11 is filled with men and women in the Bible who believed God, but perhaps my favorite New Testament walk down the Old Testament memory lane is in James 5:17–18. "Elijah was a man just like us. He prayed earnestly that it would not rain, and it did not rain on the land for three and a half years. Again he prayed, and the heavens gave rain, and the earth produced its crops." What's so special about that passage? To me, it's not that he prayed about the rain. It's those the three little words "just like us." He was just like us! He didn't have more faith, but He had a strong faith.

My son loves to lift weights to build up his muscles. When he does a bench press and lifts a potentially face-crushing barbell over his head (this is how I see it as a mother!), he has a "spotter" standing over him. The spotter's job is to catch the barbell and keep it from falling on Steven's head if Steven should slip or pick up a weight he's not strong enough to lift. As we exercise our faith, Jesus is our spotter. We might waver, and Jesus is there to make sure we don't drop the weight on our heads. We may even pick up a barbell we aren't quite ready to tackle, but it doesn't mean we give up. It simply means we keep pressing on, building up those Herculean faith muscles.

Exercise the faith you have been given. Find one promise in Scripture, confess it, believe it, and make it yours. Then pick another, then another and another. Soon that mustard seed will take root, grow tall toward the Son, sprout branches, and produce a bumper crop of fruit. God's promises are like precious gifts that He extends to His children. While we accept those gifts, we must always remember that the promises themselves are not what will change our lives, but the Promise Giver who offers and fulfills them. The psalmist reminds us that "the LORD is faithful to all his promises" (Psalm 145:13), and it is His faithfulness that brings those promises to pass.

RESTING IN FAITH

Have you ever noticed this pattern in the Gospels—the disciples get in a bind and Jesus bails them out. It reminds me of the old fifties program, *Father Knows Best.* The kids got in trouble, the father solved the problem, and he taught us all an important life lesson at the end. Come to think of it, "Father Knows Best" would be a fabulous subtitle for the Gospels!

In John 6:1–13, we find the disciples in a precarious position. Their lawn party had turned into quite a bash. The guests far exceeded their expectations, the disciples hadn't planned on providing refreshments, and it appeared the crowd was expecting dinner. But the disciples didn't have the funds or the food to feed them. All they could scrounge up were five loaves of bread and two dried fish. The crowd was getting rowdy, the disciples were getting restless, and Jesus was getting ready. He took the five loaves and two fish and told the crowd to sit down—He told them to rest.

Then He lifted the food toward heaven, blessed it, and commanded the disciples to hand out the provisions to those *who were seated.* He didn't feed people when they were running around worrying—but when they were at rest. To those He gave "immeasurably more than they could ask or imagine" (see Ephesians 3:20), with twelve baskets left over.

When we believe God, we will have rest. I want you to do something for me. Right now, I want you to use your imagination. In chapter 2 we learned that the Bible states we are in Christ and He is in us. We also learned that we are seated in the heavenlies and transferred to the kingdom of Christ. Picture yourself sitting right at Jesus' feet. Imagine Him looking into your eyes and knowing your innermost being, resting His hand upon your head and immediately accounting for each hair on your head, and meeting your gaze with a warm, affirming smile reassuring you of His love and care. Now tell me, as you picture yourself in this visual, how anxious do you feel? How rejected do you feel? How worried are you about tomorrow?

You may be thinking, "Yes, Sharon. I feel at peace in that scene. But that's not reality." Dear sister, that *is* the greater reality. What we see with our eyes is temporal. The spiritual realm, which we cannot see, is eternal.

Faith in the Storm

The most difficult times to continue believing the promises that come with your ultimate makeover are during the storms of life, storms when the waves of emotions are so great they threaten to tip your boat and spill you into an ocean of despair.

I have been there, my friend. And I do know it can be the most difficult time to believe the truth and the easiest time to believe the Enemy's lies. Let me tell about one such storm in my own life.

When my husband, Steve, and I decided to have children, we conceived with no problem. Little Steven Jr. was born with a shock of thick black hair and long Bambi-like eyelashes that had the nurses measuring for record-setting length. I loved being a mother more than any role I had ever experienced. Never had I ever imagined in my wildest dreams that so much love could be wrapped in such a small package.

Steven was about two years old when we decided to have baby number two. Conception was so easy the first time, we thought this would be a good time to share a prayer request with Steven and watch God build his faith when the prayer was answered.

"Steven," we explained, "we are going to pray that God will

give Mommy and Daddy another Jaynes baby so you can have a little brother or sister."

He thought that sounded like a good idea, so he ended our family prayer time each night with the benediction, "And God, please give Mommy and Daddy another Jaynes baby. Amen."

After six months, there was no news of another Jaynes baby. I was perplexed. Then a year passed. I was distraught. Then two years passed. I began sinking in a sea of fear and doubt. All the while, Steven prayed each night, "And God, please give Mommy and Daddy another Jaynes baby."

Steve and I began traveling down the frustrating road of doctors, infertility treatment, and timed intimacy (which is anything but intimate). Then I began worrying about how this "unanswered" prayer was going to affect Steven's faith in God. (Have you ever shared a prayer request and then wished you'd kept it to yourself?)

By age four, we still had no news for Steven. Obviously, it was not the Lord's desire for us to have another child at this time, and I didn't know how to tell Steven that we didn't have to pray that prayer *every* night. I kept hoping that he would just forget about it. But he didn't forget about it any more than he forgot the "Amen" at the end of a prayer.

So I began to pray, "Lord, please show me how to ease out of this predicament. Show me how to get Steven to stop praying for another baby so it will not damage his faith."

We had a miniature table and chairs in the kitchen where Steven and I ate lunch together each day. One day, Steven looked up, and in his sweet little voice said, "Mommy, did you ever think that maybe God only wants you to have one child?"

Shocked, I answered, "Yes, I have thought that maybe that is the case. If it is, I am so thankful, because He has given me all I have ever hoped for in a child wrapped up in one package, YOU!"

Then he turned his little head like a robin and said, "But I think what we ought to do is keep praying until you're too old to have one. Then we'll know that's His answer."

What a great idea. I had been worried about Steven's faith, but all the while, it was my own that was suffering. I was having trouble believing that God loved me. *How could He love me and withhold such a desire of my heart?* I wondered. *Maybe He doesn't love me after all.*

A favorite song Steven used to sing when he was four emphasized how big and mighty God was.

Steven didn't know how old "too old" was, but he did know that God *could* do anything. If His answer was no, he didn't have a problem with that. I told him no many times, and he understood that no did not mean "I don't love you." No just meant "no, because I know what's best for you."

The Lord taught me a great lesson through my four-year-old son. Through his childlike faith I saw an example of the attitude of trust that I should have toward my heavenly Parent, who loves me and knows what's best for me. And though the storm had subsided for just a while, a tidal wave was about to hit a few years later.

Faith in Spite of the Tidal Waves

"Steve, can you meet me for lunch? I have a little surprise I want to give to you."

I was so excited to share this unexpected news with my husband that I called him at the office and asked him to meet me at our favorite spot for lunch. After five years of infertility treatment, we had become content with the realization that it must be the Lord's desire for our son, Steven, to be raised as an only child. It appeared that he would not have a brother or sister.

And now this surprise. At lunch, as Steve opened the tiny

package containing a baby pillow wrapped in soft white tissue, he asked, "Does this mean what I think it means?"

We both blinked back tears, and all I could manage was a nod that said, "Yes, I'm pregnant."

After many years of trying to conceive, the Lord had blessed us with this unexpected pregnancy. I began planning the nursery, the doctor confirmed that the baby was growing just fine, and we were about the happiest couple on earth. But our elation was soon changed to sadness when a few months later the pregnancy ended in a miscarriage. For those of us who believe that life begins at conception, a miscarriage can be devastating, because it is not simply the loss of a child who is to be; it is the loss of a child who *is*.

I wish I could tell you I got out my Bible and began reciting the verses about my new identity. I wish I could tell you that I said, "All things work together for good" and kept my chin up. I wish I could tell you that I went into a time of prayer, trusting that "Father knows best." I did not. I went to bed and mourned for three months. I disliked sitting through church and hearing joyful people sing, my attempts at prayer seemed to bounce off the ceiling, and I allowed the tidal wave to overtake my emotions and my hope. The key was, I listened to the lies of Satan. "I told you so," he taunted.

That's when my "spotter" came and lifted the weight for me. While I couldn't pray, Jesus was praying for me (Hebrews 6:20).

One summer night, three months after the miscarriage, as I lay on my bed, crying, praying, and crying again, I wondered, *What is my child doing in heaven? What does she look like? If only I could see a glimpse of her face or have one conversation with her.* With a miscarriage there is no funeral, and there are no sympathy cards. I needed some kind of closure to this grief. Then Almighty God Himself reached down and gave me a precious gift, which lit up my darkened soul and set my whole being aglow with His love.

Just as clearly as if I were reading words on a printed page, a letter was spoken to my heart. When the words stopped coming, I jumped up and wrote each precious gift on paper.

Dear Mommy,

I asked Jesus if it would be all right for me to write you a letter. He said it would be OK.

First of all, I want to thank you for loving me and giving me life. I remember how happy you and Daddy were when you found out that you were going to have me. I remember how you prayed that I would come to know Christ at an early age. I remember how you prayed that I would have a mission in life to help others.

Mom, I know that you and Dad were sad when God decided to take me to heaven before I was born. I saw the tears that you cried. But Mom, what I want to tell you is this: Your prayers were answered. I am healthy. I am strong. I do know Christ, and He lets me sit on His lap every day. And Mom, I do have a mission. Every day new babies come to heaven who were never born. Many of them never knew the love of a mother or father. When they come to heaven, they always ask the same question; "Baby Jaynes, tell me, what was it like to have the love of a mother?" And I can tell them. Oh, how I can tell them.

Thank you, Mom, for loving me. I know you miss me. But one day we will be together, and what a time we will have. Until then, imagine me happy and whole, playing at the feet of Jesus, and telling other babies about what it feels like to have a mommy that loves them.

See you soon,
Baby Jaynes

What a precious gift the Lord had given me—not a picture of heaven seen with the eyes, but a message of comfort delivered to the heart. The time of mourning passed. I still have days when I long for this child. Some days when I look at portraits of the Jaynes threesome adorning our family room walls, I almost see a fourth shadow in the sunlight. But there will come a day when my little girl will not be a mere shadow. I will hold her in my arms. Until then, it gives me great comfort picturing her healthy and whole and being held lovingly in the arms of Christ.

During those months, I had a friend who used to sing me this song.

> God is too wise to be mistaken.
> God is too good to be unkind.
> So when you can't understand
> When you don't see His plan.
> When you can't trace His hand
> Trust His heart.[6]

Faith. It is believing God no matter what our eyes and emotions tell us. It is not enough just to know the words in our heads; we must believe them in our hearts. Faith is trusting Him in the dark. It is knowing that He is in the boat with us. He loves you, dear sister, more than you could ever know.

WHOSE REPORT WILL YOU BELIEVE?

In this book, I have mentioned some incredible truths about your ultimate makeover—who you are, what you have, and where you are in Christ. However, the Enemy has been saying and will continue to tell you quite the contrary. The question arises: Whose reports are you going to believe?

That question has reverberated throughout history. For example, the Israelites who had been freed from the Egyptian slavery in the book of Exodus faced the same dilemma. They had crossed the Red Sea and received the Ten Commandments and instructions for the tabernacle when God signaled it was time to enter the Promised Land flowing with milk and honey. He said, "Send some men to explore the land of Canaan, which I am giving to the Israelites" (Numbers 13:2).

At God's command, Moses sent in twelve men to spy out the land, and ten of them came back with this report: "We went into the land to which you sent us, and it does flow with milk and honey! Here is its fruit. But the people who live there are powerful, and the cities are fortified and very large" (Numbers 13:27–28). The men went on to say they were *like grasshoppers* compared to the giants who lived in Canaan.

However, two of the spies, Caleb and Joshua, believed God and retorted, "We should go up and take possession of the land, for we can certainly do it" (v. 30).

Guess whom the people believed? They believed the "evil report" and failed to take the land because of fear. I have an acronym for fear: False Evidence Appearing Real. They only saw the giants, but failed to see Almighty God.

God had already given them the land; the people simply had to move forward and possess it. But instead of moving into the Promised Land, they wandered in the desert for many more years. Caleb and Joshua were the only two from their generation who inhabited the Promised Land. The others died in their unbelief.

Oswald Chambers notes,

Human frailty is another thing that gets between God's words of assurance and our own words and thoughts. When we realize how feeble we are in facing difficulties, the difficulties become like giants, we become like grasshoppers, and God seems to be non-existent. But remember God's assurance to us: "I will never ... forsake you." Have we learned to sing after hearing God's keynote? Are we continually filled with enough courage to say, "The Lord is my Helper," or are we yielding to fear?[7]

I don't want to be like those Israelites who didn't believe God told the truth. Do you? Let me ask you a few questions. I have told you about some incredible promises in Scripture about who you are, what you have, and where you are in Christ. Are you going to move into the land flowing with milk and honey—take those promises and make them yours? Or, are you going to believe the evil report and continue wandering around in the desert—free from slavery, but missing the Promised Land? Whose report are you going to believe?

chapter 6

MIND MAKEOVER:

Changing the Way We Think

Several years ago, my family went on an excursion out West. We flew to Nevada, rented a car, and then proceeded to log 2,500 miles in ten days. One of our stops was Jackson Hole, Wyoming—cowboy country.

On Saturday night, we attended the local rodeo. There we sat, three city slickers among whoopin', hollerin' locals. It wasn't hard to tell the tourists from the townspeople. There were Reeboks among cowboy boots, scarves among bandannas, chewing gum among chewing tobacco, baseball caps among ten-gallon wide brim hats, and skimpy nylon windbreakers among warm fringed suede jackets. (Who knew that temperatures on a July night would plummet to 35 degrees when the sun set behind the Grand Tetons?)

The cowboys' skills entertained and amazed those of us who thought a Bronco was a four-wheel drive. Cowboys young and old rode bucking broncos, raced around barrels, and conquered angry bulls. But the most thrilling event was the lassoing contest.

The announcer introduced, "And now here's the Jackson Hole High School Lassoing champion for 1997."

My son looked at me in amazement. "They have lassoing as a school sport? They do this in P.E.?" We all sat on the edge of our seats as the cowboy waited, poised in his saddle, anticipating the calf's release from the chute. The corral door swung open and the calf burst from the gate. The cowboy, with lasso in hand, went after the bucking, twisting, galloping animal; lassoed his neck; threw him to the ground; quickly wrapped the rope around his legs; tied them securely in place; and immediately jumped up and raised his arms in victory. As the victor stood receiving his applause, his trained steed took three steps backward to secure the rope in place. "Yup, that little fella ain't goin' nowhere," the horse seemed to say.

The timer continued to run for a few seconds to make sure the calf was indeed captive. Then the cowboy's time was posted on the scoreboard. Time and time again, cowhands lassoed little calves, secured their captives, and raised their hands in victory. Only a few times did a calf escape the rope and make his way out the door on the other end.

I'll admit that I was feeling a bit sorry for the little calves, even though they were released as soon as the time was logged. But the Lord prodded my mind and told me to look and learn. Suddenly it hit me. This event was a perfect picture of what Paul described in 2 Corinthians 10:5 when he said, "We are destroying speculations and every lofty thing raised up against the knowledge of God, and we are taking every thought captive to the obedience of Christ" (NASB).

Those calves reminded me of wild and woolly thoughts that

burst forth from the chute of my mind at times: negative, rebellious, fearful, angry, worrisome, jealous; thoughts that are untamed and unruly, bucking, jumping, and running wild across pleasant plains. And my reaction should be that of the cowboy: Ride up hot on the thought's heels, lasso it, tie it up, and throw it in the dust. My response should be just like the cowboy's trusty trained horse who automatically, because of practice, takes three steps backward to make sure the negative thought "ain't goin' nowhere."

Trained because of practice. Taking every thought captive. Yes siree. Let's lasso those thoughts, sister, tie 'em up, and throw 'em back in the dust where they came from in the first place. Then we can raise our arms in victory with all the heavenly hosts applauding in victory. And believe me, the faster we do it, the better.

We need to realize there is a fierce battle going on for our minds. Let's back up to the above-mentioned verse.

> For though we live in the world, we do not wage war as the world does. The weapons we fight with are not the weapons of the world. On the contrary, they have divine power to demolish strongholds. We demolish arguments and every pretension that sets itself up against the knowledge of God, and we take captive every thought to make it obedient to Christ. (2 Corinthians 10:3–5)

This battle is not fought with hand-to-hand combat, but with spirit-to-spirit warfare. Every spiritual battle is won or lost at the beginning, right as the calf comes bursting through the shoot.

REALIZE THE ENEMY'S TRUE IDENTITY

On Tuesday morning, September 11, 2001, after I got my son off to school and my husband off to work, I took a long walk through my neighborhood. The sky was crystal clear with a gentle breeze blowing through my hair. It was a gorgeous, cool North Carolina fall day. There was nothing special on my schedule—just the ordinary. However, one hour later, because of a horrendous terrorist attack on our country in New York City and Washington, D.C., by evil personified, the day turned into anything but ordinary. I watched in horror as the television played and replayed the airplanes crashing into the World Trade Center towers and the Pentagon.

Amazingly, we never saw it coming. It started out as an ordinary day. As I thought about that, God reminded me: *That's how the Enemy always attacks—when you least expect it.*

On December 31, 1999, the world braced itself for the potentially disastrous effects of Y2K. Families and businesses alike prepared for months for what might occur as the clock ticked past 11:59 P.M. We held our breaths, clasped our hands, and braced ourselves. Yes, we were ready. What happened? Nothing. The new millennium came without incident. And yet, on an ordinary day, September 11, 2001, when we least expected, an evil force attacked our country as never before in our history.

Oh dear friends, do you see the correlation? There is an enemy in the world who seeks to kill, steal, and destroy (John 10:10). His name is Satan. He desires to destroy us just as the hijackers crashed those airplanes into and toppled the twin towers.

He has other names—the devil, the accuser of the brethren, a liar and the father of lies, the deceiver. A deceiver is someone who presents a lie in such a way that it sounds like the truth. He can make you believe something is not true when it is and make you believe something is true when it isn't. He speaks in your own voice. The thoughts feel like yours, because they are from the old you that he has memorized so well. He uses the same methods with us that he has used since the beginning of time. He's not very creative, but he is very effective.

The first step to changing the way you think is to recognize the enemy. It's not your mother; it's not your father; it's not the person who abused you as a child. The real enemy is Satan himself, and he uses your past hurts and failures as cannon fodder. If you don't have sufficient ammunition in your past, he concocts some of his own.

Once I was sitting in a group of twelve women who were telling some of their struggles from their childhood that they were having trouble letting go of. At one point, one of the ladies who had remained quiet for most of the session began to cry.

"You all have had such hardships in your life. But my childhood was wonderful. I am a terrible person and I don't have anyone to blame it on."

At that very moment, I realized that many Christians are fighting the wrong enemy. You can't win the war if you don't even realize who the enemy is. Do not be deceived. The real Enemy is the deceiver himself.

RECOGNIZE SATAN'S LIES

My neighbor, Michael, was a stand-in for Samuel, the nine-year-old son of Benjamin Martin (Mel Gibson) in the movie *The Patriot*. For months, Michael wore his hair long with extensions, slipped on Italian knickers and knee-high stockings, and acted the part of an American colonial boy. He traveled to rural South Carolina where part of the movie was taped and received an education in the production of the silver screen. Michael saw how producers and makeup artists made something not real appear as though it were. The movie was rated R for violent content, but his parents let Michael watch it upon release. The movie was a bloody, realistic reenactment of the horrors of the Revolutionary War. However, during the guts and gore, little Michael didn't even bat an eye. Why? He knew it wasn't real.

During one scene, Benjamin Martin pummeled a Union soldier and landed a hatchet square in his bloody forehead. I covered my eyes. Michael watched nonplused. His comment?

"That guy walked around on the set with that hatchet in his head for three days. We even ate lunch together and he had that hatchet with fake blood glued to his face."

Michael knew what was true, and it removed all fear. That's the power of the truth.

In 2 Corinthians 2:11 Paul says, "We are not unaware of [Satan's] schemes." So let's take a few moments and look at his battle plan. John tells us, "The one who is in you is greater than the one who is in the world" (1 John 4:4), and Paul reminds us that "in all these things we are more than conquerors through him who loved us" (Romans 8:37). But let's see how this defeated foe operates and plays with our minds so we can recognize the lies when he fires them at us.

If Satan came to you in a little red suit with a pitchfork and announced himself as the devil, you wouldn't believe a word he said. But he is cunning and disguises himself as an angel of light (2 Corinthians 11:14). When he deceived Eve, he even quoted God's words—albeit twisted and distorted. He has a collection of old tapes from your past, and he pushes rewind and play, rewind and play. Oh yes, he knows just which buttons to push. He also uses personal pronouns like "I" instead of "you." The thoughts sound something like this: "I am a failure. I am a loser. I can't do anything right. I am ugly." The thoughts sound like us, feel like us, and, before we know it, we think it is us. He did this all throughout Scripture, and he still does it today.

In 1 Chronicles 21:1, the writer notes, "Satan rose up against Israel and incited David to take a census of Israel." God had previously told David not to count his men—so wouldn't you know it, that's the very idea Satan put in his head. Of course David thought it was his own idea, but the Bible clearly states that it was not.

Satan knows exactly which lies to whisper in your ear. He has watched you over the years and is well acquainted with your insecurities, weaknesses, and vulnerabilities. Do you tend to get discouraged? He will plant seeds of discouragement in your mind. Do you tend to feel rejection and loneliness? He will put ideas that you are rejected in your mind. But are they true? No, they are not. You can do all things through Christ who gives you strength. You are loved and chosen by God. That is the truth. When we take every thought captive to the obedience of Christ, we begin to replace the lies with the truth.

As we have already established, Satan's desire is to steal your joy, rob you of the freedom which is yours in Christ, and deceive you into thinking you are still a slave to sin instead of a servant of righteousness. He wants to keep you from accepting your spiritual inheritance and keep you living like a pauper instead of a child of the King. He does not want you to believe the truth of who you are, where you are, and what you have in Christ, because he wants to keep you from being all that God wants you to be, doing all that God wants you to do, and having all that God wants you to have. I hope that makes you a little bit mad—it sure does me.

We saw in chapter 1 how he came knocking on Eve's door in Genesis 3 and sold her a bag of lies, which she bought. He then moved on to her children—especially Cain.

Cain was not a happy boy. He was angry that God had accepted his brother's sacrifice and not his. God came to Cain and confronted him about his jealousy and anger. Apparently it was written all over his face. God asked Cain, "Why are you angry? Why is your face downcast? If you do what is right, will you not be accepted? But if you do not do what is right, *sin is crouching at your door; it desires to have you,* but you must master it" (Genesis 4:7, italics added).

"The Hebrew word for 'crouching' is the same as an ancient Babylonian word referring to an evil demon crouching at the door of a building to threaten the people inside. Sin may be pictured here as just such a demon, waiting to pounce on Cain—it desired to have him."[1] Unfortunately, Cain did not master it, but let the evil thought turn into action—just like his momma did. When I think of the word *pounce,* I envision a lion ready to pounce on his prey. Interestingly, Satan is also referred to as just such an animal. "The devil prowls around like a roaring lion looking for someone to devour" (1 Peter 5:8).

The joy of the battle is that it is already won! It was won on the cross of Calvary. Satan is a defeated foe—we simply need to recognize his lies, reject them, and remind ourselves of the victory that is ours in Christ Jesus. This is not a battle to be feared. It is a battle to be recognized.

How do we begin to recognize the lies? We begin by knowing the truth—by knowing the Word of God. When bank tellers are trained to know the difference between counterfeit and real money, the instructors teach them using real money. They are taught what real money looks like—the coloring, the numbering, the markings—in order to recognize the fake. Likewise, we detect the lies of the Enemy by knowing the truth. Then if a thought comes along that doesn't match up with what the Bible says, we know it is not true. We reject the lies and replace them with truth.

REJECT THE LIES

Once I had a door-to-door vacuum salesman come to my house. To my detriment, I let him in. Before I could convince him I did not need a new vacuum, he had his demonstration trash sprinkled all over my foyer floor. Almost two hours later, I finally got him to leave. My first mistake was to let him cross the threshold of my doorway and enter my house. Once he was in, it was difficult to get him out.

It is the same way with our thoughts. Once we entertain a thought, once we allow the "salesman" to scatter his "trash" in our minds, it is hard to dismiss it or push it back out again. The place of easiest victory is at the threshold; don't even let it in the door. It has been said, "Every spiritual battle is won or lost at the threshold of the mind." I think victory is possible once the thought has passed over the threshold, but it sure will save us much heartache and pain if we begin to recognize Satan's lies and reject them from the start.

Let's go back to 2 Corinthians 10:3–5, dig deeper, and get a richer meaning of the verse by looking at the Greek definitions for the key words.

> For though we live in the world, we do not wage war as the world does. The weapons we fight with are not the weapons of the world. On the contrary, they have divine power to demolish strongholds. We demolish arguments and every pretension that sets itself up against the knowledge of God, and we take captive every thought to make it obedient to Christ.

These verses tell us that through Christ, we have the power to demolish strongholds. What is a stronghold? The Greek word for stronghold is *echo*, meaning "to hold fast." A derivation of that same word, *echuroma*, means "a stronghold, fortification, fortress." Beth Moore describes them as "anything in our lives that we hold on to that ends up holding us."[2] They are formed when thoughts or habit patterns "echo" time and time again in our lives. They are negative thoughts that are burned into our minds through repetition or a one-time traumatic incident (such as a rape). These thought patterns could grab hold of a mind and rule a life. Many are built brick by brick for protection and comfort, but they inevitably become prisons. "No matter what the stronghold may be, they all have one thing in common: Satan is fueling the mental tank with deception to keep the stronghold running."[3]

The word *demolish* implies a kind of destruction requiring tremendous power—divine power. One reason many Christians have remained in a yoke of slavery to past sins and lies of the Enemy is that they swat at strongholds as though they are mosquitoes instead of blasting them with the truth like they are concrete fortresses formed by years of construction. We cannot destroy demonic strongholds in our own strength, even on our best days. The power of the Holy Spirit can destroy strongholds even on our worst days. "The weapons we fight with are not the weapons of the world. On the contrary, they have divine power to demolish strongholds" (2 Corinthians 10:4).

The following verse goes on to describe another area that needs to be destroyed. "We demolish arguments and every pretension that sets itself up against the knowledge of God." I don't know about you, but on a few occasions (OK, on more occasions than I can count) I have argued with God and against the knowledge of God. Guess what? God always wins.

The Greek word for *arguments* is *logismos*, meaning "a reckoning, calculation, consideration, reflection." A calculated thought might be a summation that you are a failure, after you have failed at something. That seems logical. It all adds up. Upon reflection, it seems highly probable. However, that's not what the truth says. It is against the knowledge of God. Regardless of your calculations, God says you are a saint who has been blessed with every spiritual blessing in the heavenly places, a child of God, and an heir with Christ. You are not a failure, and you need to demolish that lie with the truth.

REPLACE THE LIES WITH TRUTH

Do you remember Amanda, who had the confidence makeover in chapter 4? The way she did it was to continue replacing Satan's lies with God's truth.

Satan is so audacious, he even tried to deceive God's Son with lies and cause Him to forfeit His inheritance. After Jesus had been fasting for forty days in the desert, Satan came to Him with three temptations. Just like he tempted Eve, he tempted Jesus in the three key areas of His life: His body, soul, and spirit. How did Jesus fight the Enemy? He fought him with Scripture—He fought him with the truth. Each time Satan put an evil thought before Him, Jesus said, "It is written . . ."

Although Jesus' temptations are similar to ours in nature, they were specific to His particular challenges. For example, Satan would not tempt us to turn a stone into bread, but his temptations would be customized to fit our particular struggles.

It is not a sin to be tempted. The Bible says that Jesus was tempted and yet did not sin. It becomes a sin when we act on the thought, accept it as truth, linger over it, or replay it time and again. As Martin Luther said, you can't keep the birds from flying over your head, but you can keep them from building a nest under your hat.

Let me give you this example. I believe that Satan sends us e-mails all day long (evil-mails). When we get a literal bad e-mail on the screen of our computer, is it necessarily our fault? If we get an unsolicited e-mail that reads, "Click here for a hot time tonight" is that our doing? Not unless we've placed ourselves on some bad e-mail lists. When does that e-mail become a sin? The moment we click on it and accept the invitation. Likewise, when the Enemy tempts us to believe a lie, the temptation is not sin; it becomes sin when we accept the thought as our own and act on it. Our responsibility is to delete the lie and replace it with the truth. When it comes to defeating Satan, Dr. Neil Anderson says it well: "You don't have to outshout him or outmuscle him to be free of his influence. You just have to *outtruth* him."[4]

Below are some common lies of the Enemy and the truth that "demolishes" them. I have listed each lie in first person, "I," because that is how the Enemy puts them in our thoughts.

Satan's Lie	God's Truth
I am a loser. I can't do anything right.	I can do everything through him who gives me strength. (Philippians 4:13)
Nobody loves me.	For God so loved the world that he gave His one and only Son. (John 3:16)
I'm not able to do this job. I don't have the right gifts.	Not that we are competent in ourselves to claim anything for ourselves, but our competence comes from God. He has made us competent as ministers of a new covenant. (2 Corinthians 3:5–6)
God couldn't love me.	How great is the love the Father has lavished on us, that we should be called children of God! (1 John 3:1)

Satan's Lie	God's Truth
I'm so worried about this.	Do not be anxious about anything, but in everything, by prayer and petition, with thanksgiving, present your requests to God. And the peace of God, which transcends all understanding, will guard your hearts and your minds in Christ Jesus. (Philippians 4:6)
I'm afraid I will fail.	Commit to the LORD whatever you do, and your plans will succeed. (Proverbs 16:3)
I'm so ugly.	[I have received] a crown of beauty instead of ashes. (Isaiah 61:3)
Nobody ever prays for me.	I pray for . . . those you have given me. (Jesus in John 17:9)
I'm a loser and so depressed. Nothing ever goes right for me.	God . . . has blessed us in the heavenly realms with every spiritual blessing in Christ. (Ephesians 1:3)
I can't help myself.	Resist the devil, and he will flee from you. (James 4:7)

◆ ◆

Satan's Lie	**God's Truth**
I'm all alone.	God has said, "Never will I leave you; never will I forsake you." (Hebrews 13:5)
I'm afraid of what Satan will do to me.	The evil one cannot harm [me]. (1 John 5:18)
I'm damaged goods.	[I am] a new creation; the old has gone, the new has come! (2 Corinthians 5:17)
My financial situation is hopeless.	And my God will meet all your needs according to his glorious riches in Christ Jesus. (Philippians 4:19)
	But seek first his kingdom and his righteousness, and all these things will be given to you as well. (Matthew 6:33)
I'm afraid.	Peace I leave with you; my peace I give you. I do not give to you as the world gives. Do not let your hearts be troubled and do not be afraid. (John 14:27)
	For God did not give us a spirit of timidity but a spirit of power, of love and of self-discipline. (2 Timothy 1:7)

Satan's Lie	God's Truth
I'll never get through this.	For everyone born of God overcomes the world. This is the victory that has overcome the world, even our faith. (1 John 5:4-5)
I'll never be able to get to heaven; I'm just not good enough.	It is by grace you have been saved, through faith—and this not from yourselves, it is the gift of God—not by works, so that no one can boast. (Ephesians 2:8-9)
How could God love me after all that I've done?	For he chose us in him before the creation of the world. (Ephesians 1:4)
I'm not any different. I'm just like I was before I became a Christian.	Therefore, if anyone is in Christ, he is a new creation; the old has gone, the new has come! (2 Corinthians 5:17)
I feel so empty inside.	You have been given fullness in Christ. (Colossians 2:10)
God loves me, but I don't think He likes me very much.	I have called you friends. (John 15:15)
I wish I were talented like she is.	We have different gifts, according to the grace given us. (Romans 12:6)

Satan's Lie	God's Truth
Everybody is against me.	If God is for us, who can be against us? (Romans 8:31)
I'm a mess.	For we are God's workmanship, created in Christ Jesus to do good works, which God prepared in advance for us to do. (Ephesians 2:10)
I feel so condemned.	Therefore, there is now no condemnation for those who are in Christ Jesus. (Romans 8:1)
If God loves me, how could He let this happen?	And we know that in all things God works for the good of those who love him, who have been called according to his purpose. (Romans 8:28)
I'm not having any impact on my family or my friends or the people at work.	You are the salt of the earth. . . . You are the light of the world. (Matthew 5:13-14)
I'm so depressed that I'm not married.	"Come, I will show you the bride, the wife of the Lamb." (Revelation 21:9)
I can't help it. This is just the way I am.	For we know that our old self was crucified with him so that the body of sin might be done away with, that we should no

Satan's Lie	God's Truth
	longer be slaves to sin—because anyone who has died has been freed from sin. (Romans 6:6)
No one ever chooses me.	You did not choose me, but I chose you. (John 15:16)
What I've done is unforgivable.	If we confess our sins, he is faithful and just and will forgive us our sins and purify us from all unrighteousness. (1 John 1:9)
I just don't have what it takes.	For in Christ all the fullness of the Deity lives in bodily form, and you have been given fullness in Christ, who is the head over every power and authority. (Colossians 2:9-10)
I feel like my prayers are bouncing off the ceiling.	This is the confidence we have in approaching God: that if we ask anything according to his will, he hears us. And if we know that he hears us—whatever we ask—we know that we have what we asked of him. (1 John 5:14-15)

Satan's Lie	God's Truth
I'll never get through this.	No, in all these things we are more than conquerors through him who loved us. (Romans 8:37)

I can tell you that it was very easy for me to come up with the list of lies, because I've thought most of them myself. In order to win the battle for our minds, we must refuse the lie and replace it with the truth. After all, which column is true? Annabel Gillham has a simple idea to ascertain a thought's origin. "Add 'in Jesus' name' to the end of the sentence. 'I cannot endure one more second . . . in Jesus' name. I'm such an inferior person . . . in Jesus' name. I can handle this myself. I don't need God's help . . . in Jesus' name. He doesn't love me. No one has ever loved me, and no one ever will . . . in Jesus' name.' The source of the thought is obvious once you ask Jesus to sanction it, isn't it?"[5]

Review

Let's take a moment and review the steps to changing the way we think.

- **Realize** the enemy's true identity.
- **Recognize** Satan's lies.
- **Reject** the lies.
- **Replace** the lies with truth.

Now let me add a few more steps.

- **Rely** on God to supply the feelings. Remember, emotions are the tail of the dog. Once we start acting on the truth, the tail will follow, but it might take a while. If you see a snake on the floor, on a scale of one to ten, your emotions and your mind ricochet to ten. But once you realize it is a rubber snake, your mind quickly settles back down to one while your emotions slowly settle down like a pellet in a glass of thick oil. If you've believed lies for more than thirty years, don't expect your emotions to settle back down overnight.

- **Rest** in knowing that the victory is yours. "You will keep in perfect peace him whose mind is steadfast, because he trusts in you" (Isaiah 26:3). If you make a mistake and believe a lie,
- **Repent**, tell God you're sorry, and
- **Repeat** the steps the next time.

Paul gives us a litmus test for the thoughts. "Finally, brothers, whatever is true, whatever is noble, whatever is right, whatever is pure, whatever is lovely, whatever is admirable—if anything is excellent or praiseworthy—think about such things" (Philippians 4:8). I don't know about you, but I get stuck many times right on the first one, "whatever is true." I believe if we could master thinking on the truth, the others would come naturally. Paul goes on to say in verse 9, "Whatever you have learned or received or heard from me, or seen in me—put it into practice." He knew that changing the way we think comes before changing the way we "practice" or act—thinking comes before doing.

Jesus said, "I am the way and the truth and the life" (John 14:6). He *is* truth. The more we think on truth, the more our minds will be conformed to the image of Christ, and the quicker we will recognize the lies.

My, my how beautiful you are becoming. I'd say you are actually glowing with the radiance of Christ! "Wisdom brightens a [woman's] face and changes its hard appearance" (Ecclesiastes 8:1). Stunning! Absolutely stunning!

chapter 7

EXERCISE REGIMEN:

Learning to Run like Paul

J ust the other day, I was feeling very stressed out, burned out, and fed up. I wasn't myself—I was unable to get anything done, unwilling to cooperate with my family, and unnerved by my son's behavior.

My friend Lysa called and said, "Sharon, I've been reading a book about how women between the ages of thirty-five and forty-five can feel like they are losing their mind."

"Hey, wait a minute," I said defensively.

"No, listen to this," she continued. "The author said she noticed that women in their late thirties and early forties reported major changes in their attitudes, feelings, and health. Energetic and very functional women suddenly feel hopeless and lethargic. She calls it a slump."[1]

"Lysa," I said, "I know what you are going to tell me. The author says 'exercise'!"

I have a confession to make. Under our Ping-Pong table rests an ab-rocker that hasn't rocked in about five years. In our garage a Nordic Track ski machine, bound with spider webs and coated with years of dust, lies dormant. I do not like to exercise, and yet, everywhere I turn, doctors are saying exercise, exercise, exercise! Want to increase energy level? Exercise. Want to alleviate depression and get those endorphins moving? Exercise. Want to rid yourself of unwanted pounds? Exercise. Want to sleep better at night? Exercise. Want to lower cholesterol? Exercise. Want to decrease hot flashes and mood swings? Exercise.

So you should not be surprised when I tell you that the ultimate makeover includes—what else? Exercise. I can almost hear the moans and groans now. Although I don't enjoy exercise, I've come to love the type of exercise Paul mentions in the New Testament— spiritual running!

PAUL—OUR PERSONAL TRAINER

I can't quite envision the apostle Paul at a spa or a salon, but he literally wrote the book on how to experience the ultimate makeover. To Paul, running was an important element to being conformed to the image of Christ, and he gave us some specific instructions on how to run well. He said, "Brethren, I do not regard myself as having laid hold of it yet [I am not spiritually perfect; the makeover is not finished]; but one thing I do: forgetting what lies behind and reaching forward to what lies ahead, I press on toward the goal for the prize of the upward call of God in Christ Jesus" (Philippians 3:13–14 NASB).

When my son, Steven, was in junior and senior high school, he ran cross-country in the fall and track in the spring. Fans watched on the sidelines as runners sprinted toward the finish line. When running that final stretch, the trained runners knew to never look back, but keep their eyes on the goal set before them. I frequently heard coaches yelling, "Don't look back! Don't look back!" They knew the runners who looked back lost valuable time.

In Hebrews 12:1, Paul tells us that we have a great cloud of witnesses surrounding us, cheering for us to run with endurance. I suspect if the heavenly veil that separates the seen from the unseen were lifted, we would hear Moses, Elijah, and the angels cheering for us as we run the great race of life, "Don't look back! Don't look back!"

In our society, people waste valuable, precious years looking back and trying to figure out why they are the way they are and why they do the things they do. However, Paul exhorts us to "forget it." In the Old Testament, men and women of faith did look back. However, they did so to praise God for His faithfulness, never to place blame. The psalmist said, "I shall remember the deeds of the Lord; surely I will remember Your wonders of old. I will meditate on all Your work and muse on Your deeds" (Psalm 77:11 NASB). Moses reminded the Israelites, "Remember how the LORD your God led you all the way in the desert these forty years, to humble you and to test you in order to know what was in your heart, whether or not you would keep his commands" (Deuteronomy 8:2). Again he wrote, "Remember that you were slaves in Egypt and the LORD your God redeemed you" (Deuteronomy 15:15).

As a speaker, I give my testimony often. However, I am not looking back to place blame on anyone. I am telling about my past in order to bring glory to God in the present by showing the incredible saving grace of Jesus Christ in my life and the lives of my family members.

Unfortunately, looking back trips up many spiritual runners. They stumble in the dirt because they aren't looking forward. They grovel in the dust and lose precious years because they are spending too much time looking at where they've been instead of where they are going. If I were sitting there with you, I'd cheer, "Get up! Don't look back! Keep running toward the goal! Look where you're going, not where you've been."

Paul exhorts us to leave the past behind and concentrate on moving forward in the present. When he says, "forgetting what lies behind," he describes it as involving the continual forgetting and the relentless centering of his energies and interests on the course ahead. "Forgetting" did not mean obliterating the memory of his past, but a conscious refusal to let it absorb his attention and impede his progress.[2]

What exactly did Paul have to forget? He had to forget the good, the bad, and the ugly.

Forget the Good

When I worked as a dental hygienist in my husband's office, my nametag did not have my last name engraved on it. It simply said Sharon, RDH. The other staff members used to tease me about it. But the reason I omitted my last name was to prevent patients from treating me differently from the other staff just because I was the doctor's wife. Many times, proud, highly educated or wealthy men and women snubbed me like I was just the hired help (which is exactly what I was). It always tickled me when one of them saw us together at a social function and said with embarrassment, "Oh, I didn't know you were Dr. Jaynes's wife."

The point is, it should not have mattered. I am a child of God and the status of being the "doctor's wife" was not important. As my country grandmother used to say, social status "doesn't amount to a hill of beans."

Paul had quite an impressive résumé. He was "circumcised on the eighth day, of the nation of Israel, of the tribe of Benjamin, a Hebrew of Hebrews; as to the Law, a Pharisee; as to zeal, a persecutor of the church; as to the righteousness which is in the Law, found blameless" (Philippians 3:5–6 NASB). In other words, Paul was a somebody. He was born into an elite family, studied at the Harvard of Jerusalem, and never broke a single rule. He was in the Jewish Who's Who—a real man's man.

And yet, he decided all his past credentials were rubbish in comparison to his present treasures in Christ. He said,

> But whatever was to my profit I now consider loss for the sake of Christ. What is more, I consider everything a loss compared to the surpassing greatness of knowing Christ Jesus my Lord, for whose sake I have lost all things. I consider them rubbish, that I may gain Christ and be found in him, not having a righteousness of my own that comes from the law, but that which is through faith in Christ—the righteousness that comes from God and is by faith. (Philippians 3:7–9)

I love how the Amplified version expounds on verse 8:

> Yes, furthermore, I count everything as loss compared to the possession of the priceless privilege (the overwhelming preciousness, the surpassing worth, and supreme advantage) of knowing Christ Jesus my Lord and of progressively becoming more deeply and intimately acquainted with Him [of perceiving and recognizing and understanding Him more fully and clearly]. For His sake I have lost everything and consider it all to be mere rubbish (refuse, dregs), in order that I may win (gain) Christ (the Anointed One).

God is calling us to forget our past achievements, quit wearing that letter sweater around the house, and keep moving toward the goal of becoming conformed to the image of Christ. William Barclay said, "Forget what you have done, and remember what you have to do." I think spiritual Olympian runner Paul of Tarsus would agree.

Forget the Bad

First we forget the good we have done. Second, we forget the bad that has been done to us—the cruelties, the injustices, the hurtful words, the betrayal, the slander, the abandonment, the physical or mental abuse, the rejection. We cannot change the past, but from this point on, we can ask God to change what we do with it.

Remember, forgetting does not mean obliterating something from your memory. That is physically impossible unless you have a disease such as amnesia or Alzheimer's. To forgive and forget means to no longer use the offense against the offender. It has nothing to do with whether or not the offender deserves forgiveness. Most do not. I do not deserve God's forgiveness, and yet He has forgiven me. Forgiving and forgetting is taking someone off your hook, placing him or her on God's hook, and putting the past behind you. It is a gift you give yourself.

The Greek word for "forgiveness" is *aphiemi*, and it means "to let go from one's power, possession, to let go free, let escape."[3]

> In essence, the intent of biblical forgiveness is to cut someone loose. The word picture drawn by the Greek term unforgiveness is one in which the unforgiven is roped to the back of the unforgiving. How ironic. Unforgiveness is the means by which we securely bind ourselves to that which we hate most. Therefore, the Greek meaning of forgiveness might best be demonstrated as the practice of cutting loose the person roped to your back.[4]

Author Philip Yancey, in his book *What's So Amazing About Grace?*, said, "If we do not transcend nature, we remain bound to the people we cannot forgive, led in their vise grip. This principle applies even when one party is wholly innocent and the other wholly to blame, for the innocent party will bear the wound until he or she can find a way to release it—and forgiveness is the only way."[5]

We've seen how Paul had to forget the good (putting his stellar credentials behind him), but now let's see how he had to forget the bad (the atrocities that were committed against him by others.) He recounted the cruelties in 2 Corinthians 11:23–27:

> I have worked much harder, been in prison more frequently, been flogged more severely, and been exposed to death again and again. Five times I received from the Jews the forty lashes minus one. Three times I was beaten with rods, once I was stoned, three times I was shipwrecked, I spent a night and a day in the open sea, I have been constantly on the move. I have been in danger from rivers, in danger from bandits, in danger from my own countrymen, in danger from Gentiles; in danger in the city, in danger in the country, in danger at sea; and in danger from false brothers. I have labored and toiled and have often gone without sleep; I have known hunger and thirst and have often gone without food; I have been cold and naked.

In most of Paul's writings, he makes little mention of his hardships. Honestly, if I had suffered such treatment, I probably would have brought them up often and dedicated an entire chapter to each one! But Paul chose to put the past behind him and move on.

Paul had a choice. In the face of rejection, physical abuse, and injustice, he could have chosen to become bitter and unforgiving toward those who had treated him unfairly. But instead, he chose to forgive those who had hurt him and to run the race unencumbered. I believe one of the reasons Paul may have been able to accomplish more than anyone other than Jesus Christ as recorded in the New

Testament was because of his willingness to forgive those who had hurt him.

Have you ever noticed that some of the most beautiful women with the most peaceful countenances are those who have had the most tragic lives? Corrie ten Boom was such a woman. She spent almost a year in a German concentration camp where she was humiliated and degraded by Nazi guards daily. After she was freed, she traveled around the world telling about God's grace and forgiveness through Jesus Christ. One Sunday morning, after speaking in Munich about how God throws our sins into the deepest of seas, she noticed a heavyset, balding man in a gray overcoat approaching the podium.

And as she saw the man, she pictured the uniform he used to wear—at Ravensbruck. He had been one of the most cruel guards at that place where here sister Betsie died.

He stopped in front of her and held out his hand, telling her, "A fine message, Fraulein! How good it is to know that, as you say, all our sins are at the bottom of the sea!" She hesitated and fumbled in her purse to avoid taking his hand.

He told her he had become a Christian. He knew God had forgiven her, but he wanted Corrie's forgiveness as well.

It could not have been many seconds that he stood there— hand held out—but to me it seemed hours as I wrestled with the most difficult thing I had ever had to do for I had to do it—I knew that. The message that God forgives has a prior condition: that we forgive those who have injured us. "If you do not forgive men their trespasses," Jesus says, "neither will your Father in heaven forgive your trespasses." . . .

Forgiveness is an act of the will, and the will can function regardless of the temperature of the heart. "Jesus, help me!" I prayed silently. "I can lift my hand. I can do that much. You supply the feeling."

And as she obediently raised her hand, God's forgiveness came to her heart and tears flowed to her eyes. *"I forgive you, brother!' I cried. 'With all my heart.'"*[6]

I think Corrie ten Boom never looked more beautiful than at that very moment.

Forget the Ugly

We forget the good and we forget the bad. Paul also tells us to forget the ugly things we've done, and he was a man who had some ugly to forget. Before Saul became Paul, he persecuted, arrested, and killed Christians. Saul was in charge of watching the coats while an angry mob stoned Stephen, the first Christian martyr. After he met Jesus on the road to Damascus and his name was changed to Paul, he feared the Christians would not believe that he was now one of them and would remain afraid. And yet, Paul had to put his ugly past behind him. How could he?

Later he wrote, "If anyone is in Christ, he is a new creation; the old has gone, the new has come!" (2 Corinthians 5:17). To quote from the Amplified version again, "Therefore, if any person is [ingrafted] in Christ (the Messiah), he is a new creation (a new creature altogether); the old [previous moral and spiritual condition] has passed away. Behold, the fresh and new has come!" Paul knew more than anyone the joy of new beginnings. He rejoiced that he was not the same man that he had been before he met Jesus. He had a spiritual makeover and he no longer lived, but Christ lived in him (Galatians 2:20).

Have you done some ugly things in your life that you are having trouble forgetting? Did you know that God chooses not to remember what those things are? Corrie ten Boom once said, "God casts our sins into the deepest ocean, gone forever. And even though I cannot find a Scripture for it, I believe God then places a sign out there that says, 'NO FISHING ALLOWED.'"[7]

The psalmist David wrote that God disposed of our sins as far as the east is from the west, and buried them in the depths of the sea, and yet we hop in those mental submarines and search for them on the ocean floor! I come in contact daily with women who cannot seem to fully accept God's forgiveness for their past failures. Bonnie, who had three abortions more than twenty years ago said, "I know God forgave me, but I can't forgive myself." Joan, who had an affair five years ago, said, "I know God forgave me. I understand grace, but I don't deserve forgiveness. I can't let it go."

I am convinced that two of Satan's greatest tools in his arsenal of weapons that hinder Christians from moving forward in their spiritual growth and maturity are shame and condemnation. In Revelation, Satan is called the "accuser of the brethren," and accuse he does. But the truth that will set us free says that Jesus took the punishment for us and God has declared us not guilty. When Jesus said, "It is finished" on the cross of Calvary, the words meant "paid in full." Our debt was nailed to the cross.

One reason we have difficulty forgetting past sins is that Satan is there to remind us of them on a daily basis. Bible teacher Beth Moore said, "He [Jesus] broke the chains that set the captive free, but many of us carry them in our hands or bare them dangling from our necks out of pure habit, lack of awareness, or lack of Biblical knowledge."[8] We need to throw off those chains once and for all.

It is unusual to find a woman's name in the long lists of genealogies in the Bible. However, in Jesus' lineage recorded in Matthew 1, the writer lists four women. Now, if I were going to list only four women in Jesus' family tree, perhaps I'd list Mrs.

Noah, Mrs. Moses, or Mrs. Abraham. But God had another idea. He chose Tamar, who had an incestuous relationship with her father-in-law; Rahab, who was a harlot by trade; and Bathsheba, who had an adulterous affair with King David that resulted in murder. Why would God choose three women with such sordid pasts? And why would He choose Ruth, who was a foreigner from a cursed country? I believe it was to show that there is no sin so low, no place so far, that the grace of God cannot redeem and save. In each of these women's lives, God chose her, forgave her, and used her life to glorify Him. Likewise, dear sister, there is nothing in your life that God cannot forgive, redeem, and use for His glory.

Psalm 139 assures us that God knew every day of our lives before there was yet one of them. He knew every sin we would commit and every poor choice we would make. Amazingly, He chose us anyway.

We will make mistakes, but I hope to have the attitude of Thomas Edison after a fire that destroyed his laboratory and his life's work. "Just think," he said, "all our mistakes have been burned up and we have a chance to start all over again."[9]

God forgets the ugly we've done. We need to forget too.

RUNNING WITH THE GOAL IN MIND

In the movie *Forrest Gump*, Forrest could not do many things well, but he could run. After a series of devastating circumstances, Forrest decided to start running—nowhere in particular, just run.

"That day, for no particular reason, I decided to go for a little run," he said. "I ran to the end of the road and when I got there, I thought maybe I'd run to the end of town, and when I got there, I thought maybe I'd just run across Greenbow county.... I ran clear to the ocean. When I got there, I figured since I'd gone this far, I might as well turn around and just keep on going. When I got to another ocean, I figured since I'd gone this far, I might as well just turn back and keep right on going. When I got tired, I slept. When I got hungry, I ate."

After a while, others joined Forrest in his "pursuit." A news reporter dashed up to him, stuck a microphone in his face, and asked, "Why are you running? Are you doing this for world peace? Are you doing this for the homeless? Are you running for women's rights? . . . Why are you doing this?"

Forrest replied, "I just feel like running."

Forrest had no goal. He had no direction. He had no purpose. And yet, others began to follow and run alongside him. Then suddenly, after more than three years of running, he stopped. "I'm pretty tired. Think I'll go home now." Those running with him turned to each other and questioned, "Now what are we supposed to do?"

How like the race many are running today. They run, but do not know to what end. They strive, but do not know why. Then one day, they get tired and stop. May it never be so for the Christian. We know the goal and we press on toward the prize—the ultimate makeover—conformity to the image of Christ.

Let's go back to our personal trainer's instruction: "Brethren, I do not regard myself as having laid hold of it yet; but one thing I do: forgetting what lies behind and reaching forward to what lies ahead, *I press on toward the goal* for the prize of the upward call of God in Christ Jesus" (Philippians 3:13–14 NASB, italics added). Paul is reminding us to press on toward the goal—no matter what.

Christopher Columbus understood the power of perseverance. On his journey across the Atlantic, he sailed day after day without seeing land. His crew threatened mutiny and begged him to turn back on many occasions. But Columbus pressed on, and each day he wrote two words in his ship's log, "Sailed on." There may be days when all you can write in your journal are those same two words, "Sailed on." There may be days when you feel like giving up because the monotonous repetition of everyday life threatens to lull you into complacency or the storms of life threaten to sink your ship. But be encouraged, my friend, God is at the helm. Press on.

An amazing example of pressing on toward the goal was seen in an Olympic marathon race. The crowd waited for the last of the runners to emerge.

Hours behind the runner in front of him, the last marathoner finally entered the Olympic stadium. By that time, the drama of the day's events was almost over and most of the spectators had gone home. This athlete's story, however, was still being played out.

Limping into the arena, the Tanzanian runner grimaced with every step, his knee bleeding and bandaged from an earlier fall. His ragged appearance immediately caught the attention of the remaining crowd, who cheered him on to the finish line.

Why did he stay in the race? What made him endure his injuries to the end? When asked these questions later, he replied, "My country did not send me 7,000 miles away to start the race. They sent me 7,000 miles to finish it."[10]

Dear friend, God did not choose you to merely start the race. He chose you to finish it, and finish it well. You may have skinned knees and bruised elbows from multiple falls, but just the same, there will be a cloud of witnesses cheering for you when you cross the finish line and receive your crown of glory.

What is the ultimate exercise program for the ultimate makeover? Forgetting what lies behind, reaching forward to what lies ahead, and pressing on toward the goal for the prize of the upward call of God in Christ Jesus! As Charleston Heston's director assured him during the taping of the chariot races in the movie *Ben Hur,* "You just stay in the race and I'll make sure you win." See you at the finish line!

chapter **8**

THE WEIGHT LOSS PROGRAM:

Letting Go of the Past

Maybe I left you in the dust as I talked in the last chapter about putting the past behind you. It sounds like a lovely idea, but how do you even begin to give to the Lord those burdens that you've had strapped to your back for so many years? Dear sister, I know this isn't easy. It hasn't been easy for me. But God's love will never shine through to others if the past is a dark cloud blocking the rays. Because I do understand how difficult leaving the past behind is, we are going to spend a bit more time looking at how this is done. Before we can run, we need to take some baby steps and learn how to walk.

Let's go back to the track for a moment. Imagine twenty young men lined up for a footrace. They approach the starting mark and get in position. The official calls, "On your mark," and the boys place their right feet on the white painted line. Then he calls, "Get set," and the boys reach down and strap thirty-pound packs to their backs. Some help each other secure them in place. Finally, the official fires the starting gun, yells "Go," and the runners struggle to make it down the trail, weighted down with their heavy burdens.

As foolish as this may seem, that is how many run the great race of life. However, Jesus refers to believers as sheep, and sheep are not pack animals. They were never meant to carry burdens, much less run with them.

Quite the contrary from the above scenario, when I watched my son's cross-country team prepare for a race, they stripped off long warm-up pants, slid jerseys over their heads, and put featherweight shoes on their feet. The running uniforms were so skimpy, the boys were too embarrassed to be seen in them until just minutes before the whistle was blown. But they shed the heavy sweat clothes because they understood one of Paul's greatest lessons for running well—run unencumbered. If we're not running well, perhaps we need to lose that extra weight we've been carrying around.

Paul coaches us, "Let us throw off everything that hinders and the sin that so easily entangles, and let us run with perseverance the race marked out for us" (Hebrews 12:1). The Amplified version puts it this way, "Let us strip off and throw aside every encumbrance (unnecessary weight) and that sin which so readily (deftly and cleverly) clings to and entangles us, and let us run with patient endurance and steady and active persistence the appointed course of the race that is set before us."

David said, "Cast your cares on the LORD and he will sustain you" (Psalm 55:22). Cast doesn't mean to quietly sneak up and lay the burden down. It means to get rid of it—to throw it forcefully.

The most common burden I see among God's people today is a painful past. So let's see how to strip off the past, throw it aside, and cast it at Jesus' feet.

FIND THE HIDDEN TREASURE

Several years ago, I chaperoned a group of fourth graders on a field trip to Reid Gold Mine. The tour guide took us through dark, musty tunnels, explaining how the miners one hundred years ago searched for veins of gold imbedded in the rocks and hidden beneath the mud. Many panned for years in hopes of finding a few valuable nuggets. After the tour we each grabbed a sieve and panned for gold in the mountain stream. The tour guide suggested we get comfortable, "because this might take a while."

First we lowered our pans into the mud and filled our sieves. Then we shook the pan back and forth, allowing the clear stream water to flow over its contents. The silt and dirt filtered through the screen and fell back into the stream as hopeful children (and a few adults) searched for gold. Unfortunately, none of us struck it rich that day, but I did walk away with a valuable lesson.

The first step to putting the past behind you is to find the hidden treasure in each murky situation. Just like panning for gold, we need to sift through the mud and silt, allow God's cleansing Word to wash over our memories, and discover the gold hidden beneath the surface.

One of the most valuable treasures forged from difficult life circumstances is the gift of being able to use your experience to help others. Paul said God "comforts us in all our troubles, so that we can comfort those in any trouble with the comfort we ourselves have received from God" (2 Corinthians 1:4). In other words, God does not comfort us to make us comfortable, He comforts us to make us comfort-able, able to comfort others.

Our past trials and victories give us the supernatural ability to empathize with someone going through a similar struggle. No one can help a woman who suffers from the guilt of a past abortion like the woman who has received healing and forgiveness from that same past mistake. No one can bind the open wounds left by an abusive husband or boyfriend like a woman who bears the same residual scars. No one can wipe the tears of a mother who is watching a wayward teenager make poor choices like the mother who has welcomed a prodigal home. No one can minister to a woman who feels like damaged goods because of childhood sexual abuse like the formerly abused woman who now sees herself as a holy, pure child of the King.

I see victory over hardships as a priceless treasure God has entrusted to us that we can invest into the lives of others. In the parable of the talents, a landowner went away on a trip. Before he left, he gave three of his servants talents (pieces of money). The one he gave five talents invested them and gave the owner ten upon his arrival back home. The one he gave two talents invested them and gave the owner four. But the servant who had one talent buried it in the sand out of fear he would lose it. The master was very unhappy and took the lone talent away and gave it to the first servant who had invested wisely (Matthew 25:14–28).

Victory over hardship is a treasure—a talent. I believe God is not pleased when we bury it in the sand because of fear. He is delighted when we invest those talents in the lives of others. It gives God great pleasure and Satan great frustration. The Enemy detests when we take what he meant for evil and let God use it for good.

In the book of Genesis, Joseph always seemed to find the hidden treasure in difficult circumstances. His jealous brothers could never say a kind word to him. When he was seventeen, they threw him into a pit, sold him into slavery, and told their father he was dead. Joseph was bought by Potiphar, a high official of Pharaoh, to work at his home. While there, he was falsely accused of sexually assaulting Potiphar's wife and was thrown into prison. During his prison stay, he interpreted dreams and ministered to the prisoners.

Word of Joseph's gift of interpreting dreams passed along to Pharaoh, and Joseph was called out of prison to interpret one of Pharaoh's dreams. Joseph predicted a famine in the land and was used to save the entire Egyptian nation as well as those in surrounding countries. For this, he was appointed governor.

During the famine, Joseph's brothers came to Egypt in search of food. They were terrified when the governor revealed that he was their long-lost brother. But instead of ordering their execution, Joseph forgave them and found the treasure in the situation. When he revealed his true identity to his brothers, he said, "I am your brother Joseph, whom you sold into Egypt. Now do not be grieved or angry with yourselves, because you sold me here, for God sent me before you to preserve life" (Genesis 45:4–5 NASB). After his father died and his brothers were afraid he'd take the opportunity to kill them, he reassured them, "You meant evil against me, but God meant it for good in order to bring about this present result, to preserve many people alive" (50:20 NASB). When Joseph's first son was born, he named him Manasseh, which means "one who causes to forget." He found the gold.

When putting the past behind you, discovering the treasure can soothe a wound better than any salve imaginable. The treasure may be increased knowledge of the character of God or a heightened awareness of His working in your life. It could be a character trait of your own that is sharpened or spiritual growth that could only come in the laboratory of life. The treasure might be a heightened sensitivity to the struggles of others. Like most treasure, you might have to dig through mounds of dirt before you discover it, but the eternal value is worth the effort.

Let me tell you about one of my nuggets of gold. As you recall, my husband and I struggled for many years with secondary infertility after the birth of our son. We also lost a child due to a miscarriage. I loved being a mother, and my heart ached at the thought of not having a quiver full of children. I understood when I heard someone say that she never knew she could miss someone she had never met.

Finally, one night I asked God to help me put this pain behind me and find the hidden treasure in the situation. I walked into my seven-year-old son's room, where he slept peacefully on his bed. Gently, the words of John 3:16 came to my mind. "For God so loved the world that he gave his *one and only Son*, that whoever believes in him shall not perish but have eternal life." As I whispered those words again, and looked at my child, the words *only son* resonated deep in my spirit. I had discovered the treasure.

See, I had an only son, and suddenly I had a glimpse of God's immeasurable love for me. There are many people I love a great deal, but there is no one I love enough to sacrifice my *only son*. And yet, God gave His only Son—for me. If for no other reason, I praise God for allowing me to understand more fully the magnitude of His sacrifice and the fathomless love He has for me—to give His only Son.

I found the gold.

Another way to discover the gold is to realize how God has used trials or difficulties to conform you to the image of Christ, shape your character, or remove impurities from your life. When my husband was in dental school, he learned how to melt down gold to make crowns for posterior teeth. He heated the metal and removed the dross that rose to the surface. I asked him, "Steve, what exactly is dross?"

He very professionally explained, "It is the yucky stuff that makes the gold impure."

"Yucky stuff." I like that explanation. God removes the "yucky stuff."

When a refiner works with gold, he melts it down and removes the dross or impurities. As the impurities are brought to the surface and skimmed off the top, the gold takes on a brilliant luster.

The luster is a result of the light reflecting off its pure surface—and that's what makes it beautiful. Satan wants to keep stirring up the impurities, but God wants to skim them off the top.

Job was a man who had experienced a deluge of adversity. He had suffered the loss of his children, his livestock (livelihood), and his health. In Job 23:10 he stated, "But he [God] knows the way that I take; when he has tested me, I will come forth as gold."

God allows trials, and He will use them to remove the "dross," the "yucky stuff" that blocks the reflection of His character in our lives. Conformity to the image of Christ is rarely comfortable. Sometimes God has to turn up the heat. But the end product can be 100 percent gold bullion.

"And all of us have had that veil removed so that we can be mirrors that brightly reflect the glory of the Lord. And as the Spirit of the Lord works within us, we become more and more like him and reflect his glory even more" (2 Corinthians 3:18 NLT).

As my country grandmother used to say, "You're just gettin' purdier and purdier all the time."

FORGIVE THOSE WHO HURT YOU

C. S. Lewis said, "Everyone says forgiveness is a lovely idea until they have something to forgive."[1] Perhaps the most difficult facet of forgetting the past is forgiving those who have hurt you. But forgiveness is more about what you do than what was done to you.

Unforgiveness is a trap, a net, and a snare. It will trap you like a fly in a spider's web, and it will suck the very life from your soul. Paul warns us of this trap. "If you forgive anyone, I also forgive him. And what I have forgiven—if there was anything to forgive—I have forgiven in the sight of Christ for your sake, in order that Satan might not outwit us. For we are not unaware of his schemes" (2 Corinthians 2:10-11).

We are warned that unforgiveness also causes a root of bitterness to grow deep into our souls (Hebrews 12:15). Henry and Richard Blackaby explain this well.

> Bitterness has a tenacious way of taking root deep within the soul and resisting all efforts to weed it out. . . . Time, rather than diminishing the hurt, only seems to sharpen the pain. . . . You find yourself rehearsing the offense over and over again, each time driving the root of bitterness deeper within your soul. . . . Bitterness is easy to justify. You can get so used to a bitter heart that you are even comfortable with it, but it will destroy you. Only God is fully aware of its destructive potential.[2]

Malcolm Smith gives this analogy.

> We find some perverse joy in licking old wounds. We return to the hurts again and again, reliving them in a movie we play in the theater of our minds . . . a movie in which we are the stars. We see ourselves abused, wronged—but oh so right. Every time we play this movie in our imagination we bear again what each person said or didn't say, what was done, and how it was done. We cling to our memories because in our darkened minds we believe that if we forget, the one who hurt us may go free! . . . Bitterness arises from the belief that the person who hurt us owes us and must somehow pay us back.[3]

Amazingly, many times the person we are holding a grudge against isn't even aware of it or doesn't care about the ill feelings. Ultimately, the only person being hurt is the person refusing to forgive. In essence, when we don't forgive, it is like we are trying to punish the person by banging our own heads against the wall and saying, "Here, take that!" As I mentioned before, perhaps the person doesn't *deserve* to be forgiven. Perhaps you don't want to let the offender off the hook. None of us deserves to be forgiven, but look at how God forgave you and me. If we got what we deserved, we would all be sentenced to eternity in hell. But God gives us grace (receiving what we don't deserve) and mercy (not receiving what we do deserve).

When you let someone off of your hook and place him or her on God's hook, you will be free. It doesn't mean what the person did was not wrong. It does mean that you are no longer going to let the memory of it hold you captive. It means that you are no longer going to use the person's sin against him or her.

How much do we forgive? How many times? Is there any offense that warrants unforgiveness? In Matthew 18:21–22, Peter asked Jesus, "Lord, how many times shall I forgive my brother when he sins against me? Up to seven times?"

Jesus answered, "I tell you, not seven times, but seventy-seven times."

Sometimes I think I like Peter's ideas better—seven strikes and you're out, buddy. But Jesus tells us to put no limit on forgiveness. He even gives us a story to drive the point home.

> Therefore, the kingdom of heaven is like a king who wanted to settle accounts with his servants. As he began the settlement, a man who owed him ten thousand talents was brought to him. Since he was not able to pay, the master ordered that he and his wife and his children and all that he had be sold to repay the debt. The servant fell on his knees before him. "Be patient with me," he begged, "and I will pay back everything." The servant's master took pity on him, canceled the debt and let him go. But when that servant went out, he found one of his fellow servants who owed him a hundred denarii. He grabbed him and began to choke him. "Pay back what you owe me!" he demanded. His fellow servant

fell to his knees and begged him, "Be patient with me, and I will pay you back." But he refused. Instead, he went off and had the man thrown into prison until he could pay the debt. When the other servants saw what had happened, they were greatly distressed and went and told their master everything that had happened. Then the master called the servant in. "You wicked servant," he said, "I canceled all that debt of yours because you begged me to. Shouldn't you have had mercy on your fellow servant just as I had on you?" In anger his master turned him over to the jailers to be tortured, until he should pay back all he owed. This is how my heavenly Father will treat each of you unless you forgive your brother from your heart. (Matthew 18:23–35)

The first servant was forgiven a debt that would amount to millions of dollars by today's standards, and yet he refused to forgive a debt that would be equivalent to just a few thousand dollars. God is the king, and He has forgiven me of so much. How can I not forgive others who have hurt me?

God's forgiveness should stir such love in us that we long to forgive others in return. In Luke 7:36–50, a prostitute came to Jesus while He dined with a Pharisee. She wept, washed His feet with her tears, dried them with her hair, and anointed them with perfume. She was overcome with Christ's love and forgiveness. When the Pharisees questioned her acts, Jesus reminded them, "He who has been forgiven little loves little." She had been forgiven much — and, as a result, loved much.

Back to our friend Joseph. Chuck Swindoll notes that "Joseph blazes a new trail through a jungle of mistreatment, false accusations, undeserved punishment, and gross misunderstanding. He exemplifies forgiveness, freedom from bitterness, and an unbelievable positive attitude toward those who had done him harm.

He forgave those who had harmed him and made sure bitterness never had a chance to take root."[4]

Are you harboring unforgiveness in your heart? Remember the word picture I drew of the boys preparing to run the race with a heavy backpack strapped on each of their backs? Remember the word picture in Scripture of unforgiveness being someone strapped to your back—strapping the person you can't forgive to your very being? Lugging the person around day after day? Is there someone strapped to your back? Most likely some of us have an entire busload of folks tied on there. No wonder we find the "great race of life" tiring and cumbersome! God never intended us to run with such a load!

If you have someone strapped on your back, nothing in this book, no spiritual beauty treatment available, can erase the marring effects of unforgiveness on your soul. I have to tell you, as I write this book, every time I type the word "unforgiveness" my spell checker underlines it in red to show that it is not a word. That's what Satan would have us believe. He would have us believe that unforgiveness is not a word and unforgiveness is not a problem. Believe me, it is very real, and if left untended, it can destroy your life.

Perhaps you are unsure if you have unforgiveness in your heart. Perhaps the unforgiveness has been in your heart so long, it feels at home—like it belongs there.

"We cannot drop chains we don't even know we are carrying."[5] Stop and pray Psalm 139:23-24, "Search me, O God, and know my heart; test me and know my anxious thoughts. See if there is any offensive way in me, and lead me in the way everlasting." Let me tell how that prayer changed my life.

After my sophomore year in college, I decided to take a break and work for a year or so. After the first year, I felt God was calling me to return to school, but it seemed an invisible force was holding me back. Plans were not falling into place, I was confused about where to go, and I could not get clear direction or peace from the Lord. Not to decide is to decide, so I stayed at my job another year.

When the second spring came around, my desire to return to school resurfaced. The confusion about what to do and where to go resurfaced as well. At the same time, I began having flashbacks of forgotten violent childhood memories.

I went to visit Mr. Thorp, a man who had been a spiritual mentor to me during my teenage years. I told him about my confusion about college and about the flashbacks. Mr. Thorp decided that we should read some Scripture about prayer before we prayed together for God's direction.

First he turned to Matthew 6:8–15:

For your Father knows what you need before you ask him. This, then, is how you should pray: "Our Father in heaven, hallowed be your name, your kingdom come, your will be done on earth as it is in heaven. Give us today our daily bread. Forgive us our debts, as we also have forgiven our debtors. And lead us not into temptation, but deliver us from the evil one." For if you forgive men when they sin against you, your heavenly Father will also forgive you. But if you do not forgive men their sins, your Father will not forgive your sins.

Then he turned to Matthew 18:19–22:

"Again, I tell you that if two of you on earth agree about anything you ask for, it will be done for you by my Father in heaven. For where two or three come together in my name, there am I with them."

Then Peter came to Jesus and asked, "Lord, how many times

shall I forgive my brother when he sins against me? Up to seven times?"

Jesus answered, "I tell you, not seven times, but seventy-seven times."

Each time Mr. Thorp turned to a passage about God answering prayer, there was one about forgiveness embracing it either before or after.

"Sharon," he said, "I sense that God is telling you that you have unforgiveness toward your father. Is that true?"

I wanted to say, "Wait a minute. I came here to ask for prayer about my future, not about my past." But God was showing me that unforgiveness in my past was impeding His work in my future.

At that time in my life, I had been a Christian for seven years. My father had become a Christian just a year before. I did not even realize that I had not forgiven him for the pain he had caused in my childhood. Now, when he made a mistake, all those old feelings I had toward him resurfaced. I knew that God was telling me that in order for my life to move forward in the future, I had to forgive the past.

That night, I forgave my father for everything he had ever done. When I did, God set me free, and my life moved to a new and deeper level with Him. Interestingly, the next day, the cloud of confusion lifted. I applied to college in late spring, even though the head of the department told me it was too late and the program I desired to enroll in was full. They told me the only way I could get in was if someone were to drop out—which was very unlikely. Confident that this was God's plan for me, I resigned from my job and looked for an apartment near the college campus. Ten days before the start of the fall semester, the head of the department called and said, "You won't believe this, this never happens, but someone just dropped out. We'd like you to come in the fall if you can make the arrangements."

I could believe it, and the arrangements were already made. I enrolled in the fall and met my husband four weeks later. Nine months later, I became his wife.

I am not saying that when you offer forgiveness, you'll strike it rich, find the man of your dreams, or live happily ever after. However, I do believe that unforgiveness can block God's power in our lives and cause us to miss out on a storehouse of blessings.

I was in bondage for many years because of unforgiveness. Hear me here, it was bondage. I was held captive. But as Beth Moore states, "I never knew I was in bondage until Jesus began to set me free."[6]

In counseling sessions, Dr. Neil Anderson asks patients to make a list of those who have offended them. Ninety-six percent put father and mother as number one and two.[7] I did not realize how easy it was to be in that one or two position until I had a child of my own. Yes, my parents made mistakes. I, as Steven's mother, have made mistakes. Steven, when he becomes a father, will make mistakes. The only perfect parent is our heavenly Father.

ACCEPT GOD'S FORGIVENESS

The apostle John wrote, "If we confess our sins, he is faithful and just and will forgive us our sins and purify us from all unrighteousness" (1 John 1:9). God promises to forgive us our sins, and Satan promises to remind us of our sins in order to prevent us from feeling forgiven. Whom are you going to believe?

All God requires in order for us to receive forgiveness is repentance. Repentance is agreeing with God about our sins and turning to go in the opposite direction. However, repentance and forgiveness do not always remove the consequences of our sin. God forgave David for adultery and murder; however, his firstborn son from that union still died as a result (2 Samuel 12:14). Abraham was wrong to sleep with Hagar instead of waiting on God to provide a son through his wife, Sarah. God forgave Abraham, but as a result of his sin, the Jewish and Arab nations are still at war today. He forgives sexual sin today, but unplanned pregnancies, sexually transmitted diseases, and alienated family members may be the consequences that are the natural outgrowth of such choices.

F. B. Meyer wrote:

> Learn to forget . . . and do not dwell upon past sin. There may be things in our past of which we are ashamed, which might haunt us, which might cut the sinews of our strength. But if we have handed them over to God in confession and faith, He has put them away and forgotten them. Forget them, and . . . the sin which has vitiated and blackened your record, [and] reach forward to realize the beauty of Jesus.[8]

When Joseph's brothers came to the governor of Egypt for grain during the time of famine, only to discover the governor was the brother they had sold into slavery, I am sure they were filled with guilt and remorse. However, Joseph encouraged them to forgive themselves by saying, "And now, do not be distressed and do not be angry with yourselves for selling me here, because it was to save lives that God sent me ahead of you" (Genesis 45:5). Interestingly, the brothers were brought back to Joseph after their initial visit partly because Joseph had hidden a treasure in their saddlebags. When they came back to the governor, he exchanged that hidden treasure for a much more valuable one—forgiveness.

When I was a counselor at a crisis pregnancy center, a woman came in because of depression she felt every spring. During a session, she confessed that she had an abortion on April 5 at 10:30 A.M.

more than ten years before. Now each year around April 5 she sank into a depression. Susan was now a Christian, and had asked God to forgive her, but had failed to fully accept His forgiveness. She left Satan holding the trump card, and he played it every spring. Through counseling in God's Word, she was finally able to be free from her past.

At Proverbs 31 Ministries, we occasionally teach home organization seminars. I always tell women to gather three bags when cleaning out a closet: a give away bag, a throw away bag, and a put away bag. I also tell them it is very important to use bags that they cannot see through. Why? Because it is human nature to go back through the trash and start pulling things back out. Suddenly, that old belt doesn't look so bad anymore. And what was I thinking when I put that sweater in the give away bag!

Friend, accept God's forgiveness, forgive yourself, and for goodness' sakes, don't go back through the trash. You don't want it, God has already disposed of it, and it's not worth having.

A Woman Who Put the Past Behind Her

Cary was a woman who experienced a dramatic makeover once she learned the steps to forgetting the past. Cary lived with her father, mother, and two older brothers in a simple bungalow with concrete floors, no running water, and an outhouse in the backyard. Although her father was a cold, violent man, her mother was very loving and kind. Her earliest memory is when she was three years old. Her parents had a violent argument in which her dad punched a gaping hole in the den wall and then screeched out of the driveway in his car, abandoning the family. When Cary was four years old, her father returned, beat up her mother, ripped her children out of her arms, and forced them into his car.

"You can't take care of these children," he yelled. "You can't even drive a car. I've got a new wife who'll look after them better than you can. I'm taking them, and there's nothing you can do about it."

Cary's mother believed him and didn't try to get them back. Cary remembers her mother's battered face standing in the doorway crying, "At least leave me my baby girl." Cary's heart broke as her father drove out of the driveway and away from her world. Cary's new stepmother was a cold, hard woman who showed little to no affection to her husband's three children. The trio lived for the weekends when they could go "home" and visit their mother.

Shortly after Cary arrived at her father's home, he began sexually abusing her. Confused and afraid, Cary began wearing two to three pairs of pajamas and even using safety pins to hold them together. Still her father violated his daughter time and time again.

Cary's brothers missed their mother terribly. She had married again, to a violent alcoholic, and they constantly worried about her safety. At night, when their father and stepmother went out to dinner or to a movie, the boys called their mother's next-door neighbor. Their mother didn't have a telephone, so the neighbor ran to get her so she could talk to her children. One night, the call brought some news that shattered their world forever.

"Hi, this is Allen and Bobby. Can you go get our mom?"

"I'm sorry, boys. Didn't someone tell you? Your mom's husband shot her in the back today and then killed himself. Your mother's dead."

The one person who loved Cary the most was gone forever.

The sexual abuse continued. When Cary was fourteen years old, she locked her door. The next day, her enraged father took the door off its hinges and Cary lost all privacy or protection.

When Cary was sixteen years old, her father was in a car accident that caused him to be home during the day. Summer was approaching, and Cary was terrified of what he would do to her on the long summer days. Finally, she gathered the courage to tell the authorities. They promised they would come and get her, but they never did. In desperation, she called the school guidance counselor and begged him to rescue her from this twelve-year nightmare. The counselor did come, but because he did not know where to take her, she was placed in a juvenile detention center. The center was filled with girls who were being punished and one girl who was being protected—Cary.

The weeks Cary spent at the detention center were the most secure ones of her young life. Bars kept the girls in, and bars kept Cary safe. One Sunday, a Baptist preacher came to the detention center and presented the gospel of Jesus Christ. At last, Cary heard that someone loved her. At the close of the service, he asked, "If anyone would like to accept Jesus as their personal Savior, please stand." With tears streaming down her cheeks, Cary stood.

Three weeks after Cary's arrival at the center, an aunt who lived on the West Coast came and took her to live with her and her husband. Eventually, they adopted her as their own child. Cary believed that she now had a chance to see what a real family was like. That dream was quickly shattered.

Cary adored her uncle and trusted him with all her heart. However, he destroyed that trust when he made sexual advances toward her two years after her arrival. Once again, a father figure violated her. Only this time, Cary knew she could have said no, but didn't. She felt dirty, ashamed, and worthless. Cary went off to college, and like the woman at the well, tried to fill her emptiness the only way she knew how, with men. She married at eighteen, but had it annulled six months later. She married again at twenty, but divorced after six years. She married again at twenty-six, and divorced after fourteen years. She married again at forty, but divorced three years later.

One night, she met Jesus at the well. She opened up her Bible in search of verses on joy. *Surely the Bible can tell me how to find real joy,* she thought.

She turned to Psalm 16:11, "You will fill me with joy in your presence." Then to Romans 4:7-8, "Blessed are they whose transgressions are forgiven, whose sins are covered. Blessed is the man whose sin the Lord will never count against him." She flipped to John 15:11-12, "I have told you this so that my joy may be in you and that your joy may be complete. My command is this: Love each other as I have loved you." Then to 1 John 1:9, "If we confess our sins, he is faithful and just and will forgive us our sins and purify us from all unrighteousness."

The Holy Spirit opened her eyes to the truth that would set her free. "God, are you telling me that in order to find happiness, I must forgive?"

One by one, Cary began to pray and forgive those who had hurt her. "Lord, I forgive my father for abusing me. I forgive my stepmother for not protecting me. I forgive Jake for killing my mother. I forgive Uncle James for seducing me." With each person Cary forgave, she felt a release as if the shackles of oppression were dropping from her arms, legs, and heart.

When I met Cary at a women's retreat, she listened intently as I spoke about running the race like Paul. "We must forget the past: the good that we've done, the bad that others have done to us, and the ugly that was done by us," she heard me say. "We must find the hidden treasure, forgive those who have hurt us, and forgive ourselves."

See, there was one person Cary had not forgiven—herself. Yes, she had made a series of bad choices throughout her life and Satan reminded her of them daily. Finally, on a Saturday, in March 2000, Cary decided to stop listening to the voice of the accuser and believe the truth in 1 John 1:9. That day, Cary fully accepted God's forgiveness and was finally free.

Today, Cary is running the great race of life unencumbered. And like the woman at the well, she has left her water pot and brought an entire community to the Man who told her about the living water that quenches so we will never thirst again. Today she is a speaker and Bible teacher who shares God's freeing truths with all who will listen. She has found the gold by using her past experiences to lead them to the one who sets the captive free.

Your Invitation to Freedom

North Carolina has birthed some very influential men and women. Perhaps one of our favorites is Andy Griffith of *The Andy Griffith Show*. In Andy's fictional town of Mayberry lived a town drunk named Otis. When Otis was arrested for public drunkenness, Andy put him a jail cell until he sobered up. After a good night's sleep, Otis would wake up, stick his hand through the bars of the jail cell door, take the key from a nail hanging on the wall, and let himself out. It was just that simple. On a few occasions, Otis stumbled into the jail house and locked himself in the cell, placing the key back on the nail on the wall.

This was always a comical scene, but it reminds me of the jail we lock ourselves in when we remain a prisoner to our pasts. The key is within reach. Will you be free?

chapter 9

A BRAND NEW WARDROBE:

Replacing Rags with a Royal Robe

Her daddy called her his *little princess*—not just because she looked like one, but because she actually was one. Tara's daddy was the king and she was indeed his little princess. Her name meant Palm Tree, a symbol of victory and honor. But as we all know, being born into a wealthy prestigious family does not ensure a peaceful, happy life devoid of heartache, tragedy, and despair. Thus was the case for Tara.

Tara had several siblings: brothers, half-brothers, sisters, and half-sisters. It was a royal blended mess. One half-brother in particular made her feel very uncomfortable. Aaron stood too close to her when he spoke, held her a bit too long when they greeted each other with a hug, and complimented her with a gleam in his eye that did not seem quite brotherly. On many occasions at the dinner table, she felt his eyes burning a hole right through her. When she dared meet his gaze, he smiled a toothy wicked grin that sent chills down her spine. Being in his presence made her feel as though she had walked through a spider web and left her trying to wipe away an invisible netting that clung to her soul.

One day Tara mentioned her uneasiness to her sister. "Oh, that is just his flirtatious personality," her sister chided. "Besides, what makes you think he would be interested in you? It's only your imagination, silly girl."

Tara was not imagining her half-brother's infatuation. Aaron lusted after Tara both day and night. His passionate longings were so consuming that a friend noticed his frustration.

"What's wrong with you, Aaron?" his friend asked. "Why do you look so haggard morning after morning?"

"I can't get any sleep," Aaron answered. "All I can think about is getting Tara into my bed."

The friend's pulse quickened at the mere mention of Tara. She was indeed beautiful in form and face. "You are a prince, aren't you? Here's what you need to do" . . . and the two of them devised an evil plan.

The next day, Aaron pretended to be sick in his bed. When his father came to check on him, he said, "Dad, I don't feel well, and the only food that sounds good to me is some of Tara's sweet rolls. Would you please ask her to bring some to my room?"

At her father's request, Tara brought Aaron a plate of freshly baked bread still warm from the oven. But it was not the delicious aroma of Tara's cooking that caused Aaron's senses to stir. When Tara approached his bed, he quickly commanded all the servants to leave the room and close the door behind them. The young girl dropped the plate and froze in fear. Aaron grabbed his sister and threw her across his satin sheets.

She wrestled, fought, and pounded on her half-brother's chest and face and arms, but the struggle only seemed to make him more aroused and passionate. She was no match for his strength and determination. In less than ten minutes, Tara lost her most precious commodity, her virginity.

After Aaron's obsession had been satisfied, he pushed his sister onto the floor in disgust. Now he hated her more than he had ever loved her.

Tara fled from Aaron's bedroom with tears streaming down her cheeks and blood trickling from the corner of her mouth. She tore off the royal robe of a virgin princess and wailed through the castle halls looking for her best friend, her brother Alexander. Alexander heard her cries, ran to meet her with a fatherly embrace, and swore to get even. "Shhhhhh," he said, holding his index finger to his lips. "Don't tell anyone this has happened. Come and live at my house for a while."

Tara was inconsolable and spent the rest of her days in darkened desolation and isolation at Alexander's home. She never again put on the royal robes of a princess, but wore only the rags of a lowly chambermaid.

This story reads like it could be from the pages of the *National Enquirer* or from a made-for-TV movie or an afternoon soap opera. Although I have embellished the details, the story is from 2 Samuel 13 in the Bible and tells the sordid tale of three of King David's children. Tara is Tamar; Aaron is Amnon; and Alexander is Absalom.

Tamar's story may be your story. If you have ever been sexually or emotionally abused, you have something in common with Tamar. If you have ever been shamed or rejected, you have something in common with Tamar. If something despicable has ever happened to you and others advised you not to tell, you have something in common with Tamar. If you have ever felt unprotected by your earthly father, you have something in common with Tamar.

If you have lived in mourning and desolation, you have something in common with Tamar. But no matter what your particular situation may be, there is one thing you do not have in common with Tamar. Tamar's daddy left her in sackcloth and ashes and didn't do anything to restore her to her rightful position. Your Daddy has made a supreme sacrifice to give you a new wardrobe and place you back in the royal court.

THE ORIGINAL WARDROBE

When I was ten years old, my grandmother started me on a journey of learning how to sew. Our first project together was to transform a rectangular piece of fabric into a nicely gathered apron with two front pockets and an ample sash that tied around my tiny waist. The first article of clothing young Eve crafted in the Garden of Eden was an apron as well.

Let's go back to the Garden and peek into Eve's sewing room. When Eve and Adam disobeyed God and ate the fruit, their eyes were opened; they saw their nakedness and ushered in two new emotions: fear and shame. In an effort to cover their shame, Eve devised a needle and thread of sorts and sewed fig leaves together to make "aprons." Some translations of the Bible call them "coverings" (Genesis 3:7 NIV) or "loin coverings" (NASB). But the best translation is in the King James Version, "aprons." The Eve original just covered front and center—only the part she could see.

Just as Eve tried to camouflage her shame with an apron, we still tend to try to cover our shame with modern day aprons. But there's one thing about an apron—especially if it is the only thing you're wearing—it doesn't cover your backside. I'm sure as soon as Adam and Eve turned to walk away Satan snickered at the sight.

Have you ever made an apron to cover your shame? Maybe not a literal apron, but some other type of modern day fig leaves.

Women don't even wear aprons much these days, but perhaps we try to cover our shame with beautiful clothes, a perfectly decorated home, or good works.

The only time I ever wear a real apron is when I'm working. Have you ever tried to cover your shame by "working for the Lord," trying to become acceptable by serving, doing, and attempting to please everyone? If we are hiding behind aprons, we might fool some of the people some of the time, but sooner or later we're going to have to walk away—and look out for what's exposed!

God saw Adam and Eve's pitiful aprons (and their backsides) and knew their feeble attempt at covering their disobedience was insufficient. So He killed an animal, made garments of skin and clothed them—front and back. This was probably the first blood sacrifice for sin and a foreshadowing of the sacrifice of Christ that was to come. Although this covering provided a temporary covering of their shame, God devised another plan to cover man's shame once and for all. He provided another sacrifice, His one and only Son, Jesus Christ. Because of Jesus' death on the cross and resurrection from the dead, our sins have been covered by His blood. When we accept Christ as our Savior, one of the benefits of becoming a child of God is receiving a new wardrobe. We are clothed with Christ's righteousness. We are clothed with Christ Himself (Galatians 3:26–27).

One of the best word pictures of being clothed with Christ that I have seen in my mind's eye is found in the book of Judges. When God called the cowardly Gideon to become the leader of the Israelite army, the Bible says, "the Spirit of the Lord came upon Gideon" (Judges 6:34). The Hebrew word for "came upon" is *labesh*, which means "wrap around, put on a garment or clothes."[1] One Interlinear Bible notes it this way, "and the Spirit of Jehovah clothed Gideon with Himself." Isn't that a wonderful picture of God wrapping Gideon in Himself? Can you imagine? You should, because you have also been clothed with Christ in the same way. It's a perfect fit. Jesus bet His life on it.

One of the results of the exercise program (learning to run like Paul) and the weight loss program (releasing your burdens to the Lord) is the need for a new wardrobe. If you have ever had a dramatic weight loss, you know the excitement of having to purchase new clothes to fit your new look! In the ultimate makeover, God has purchased a new wardrobe for you, and He's waiting to place it on your shoulders.

A ROBE OF RIGHTEOUSNESS

Through my work in ministry to women, I meet many who suffer needlessly just like Tamar. Oh, they may not be walking around with ashes on their heads or dressed in sackcloth, but they wear the mantle of shame that Satan has placed on their shoulders and secured with deception. They may have children, a husband, and a successful career, and look beautiful on the outside, but many are spending their days in desolation of the soul because Satan has convinced them that's where they deserve to stay. Wearing the cloak of shame because of past abuse, misuse, or mistakes, they don't realize that Jesus Christ has purchased a robe of righteousness for them and He's eager to place it on their shoulders. Perhaps you are one of these women who needs to change her wardrobe.

Let's go back to Tamar for a moment. Let's pretend the story didn't end as it did in 2 Samuel 18. Dream with me, if you will. . . .

Tamar had lived in desolation and isolation for many years. Her body was frail from lack of appetite and exercise. Her arms and legs were calloused and raw because of the never-ending rubbing of the burlap over her once smooth skin. The ashes had worked their way into her pores so that she had the ashen gray appearance of death. No one in her brother's household had been able to console Tamar. After a while, they simply tired of trying.

One day, she was awakened from her trance as her bedroom door creaked open and a stream of light burst into the room. Standing in the doorframe was the figure of a man she did not recognize but who yet seemed familiar. The light followed Him as He approached her as if it was emanating from His body instead of some outside source. He was dressed in a shimmering white robe and looked like the Son of God. She dared not meet his gaze, but hid her head in the shame that had become her signature cloak.

"Do not be afraid, My precious one," He spoke softly. "My Father, the King of heaven and earth, has sent Me to you."

Tamar could not bear to raise her eyes to meet His, so He placed His hand under her chin and gently lifted her head. Their eyes locked and she felt warmth run over her chilled body. With His thumb, He wiped away a tear that trickled down her cheek and cupped her face in His hands. Such love and compassion she had never known.

After what seemed like an eternity, He held out His hand and Tamar fit hers into His palm. When she did, she noticed a scar in the palm of His hand the size of a large nail, and her name engraved directly under it. Without saying a word, He dipped a cloth into His side and washed her with His blood. Beginning at her head and ending at her toes, the years of soot and filth began to disappear and Tamar's skin shone white and pure as a newborn babe. Not only was her skin clean and pure, but her sackcloth had been transformed into a royal robe more beautiful than the ones she had worn in her father's court.

He looked deeply into Tamar's eyes and whispered, "I have come to bind up the brokenhearted, to proclaim freedom for the captives and release from darkness for the prisoners. To comfort all who mourn, and provide for those who grieve, to bestow on them a crown of beauty instead of ashes, the oil of gladness instead of mourning, and a garment of praise instead of a spirit of despair" (see Isaiah 61:1–3).

Tamar had never felt freer in all her life. No more shame. No more despair. Suddenly she began to sing a song she had heard her father play on his harp many years ago: "You removed my sackcloth and clothed me with joy" (Psalm 30:11). "I delight greatly in the LORD; my soul rejoices in my God. For he has clothed me with garments of salvation and arrayed me in a robe of righteousness" (Isaiah 61:10).

Jesus added His own song of promise. "Those who look to him are radiant; their faces are never covered with shame" (Psalm 34:5).

It was then that they danced.

Dear sister, when your heavenly Father looks at you, He sees you clothed in Jesus Christ—pure, holy, and spotless. Don't let Satan convince you to put back on the sackcloth of shame. God has provided a new wardrobe, and we need never wear those old hand-me-downs again!

chapter 10

EXFOLIATE THE OLD:

Getting Rid of Unholy Habits

Of all the activities ten-year-old Miriam enjoyed, she loved riding horses the best. Charlie, her favorite horse, had a sleek chestnut mane, well-defined muscular legs, and a fierce strong will to match. Miriam felt powerful and self-assured when controlling this massive animal—except, that is, when he caught a glimpse of the barn. Whenever Miriam and Charlie returned from a jaunt in the woods, as soon as they got close enough for him to see the barn, he bolted homeward, forcing Miriam to hang on to the reins for dear life.

One day, Miriam's riding instructor witnessed this strong-willed animal taking control of his mistress. She was indignant.

"Miriam! What are you doing?" she called out. "You cannot let that animal control you in that manner! Bring that horse back out of the barn this instant."

Dutifully, Miriam mounted Charlie and rode him a distance away from the stalls.

"Now," the wiser, older woman instructed, "when you turn around and Charlie sees the barn and begins to run toward it, turn your reins all the way to the right. Do not let him go forward."

On cue, Miriam steered her horse toward the stalls. On cue, he began to bolt.

"Turn him! Turn him!" the instructor shouted.

Young Miriam pulled the reins to the right as hard as she could until the horse's head was inches away from touching his right shoulder. But instead of obeying her lead, Charlie fought her with the force of a war horse. Round and round the horse and rider circled.

"Don't let go," the instructor shouted. "You must break his will!"

After ten long minutes of going in circles, Miriam and Charlie grew exhausted and quite dizzy. He stopped circling. She stopped pulling him to the right.

"Now gently tap him to see if he will walk toward the barn instead of run," the instructor commanded.

Charlie did not bolt, but walked at a steady pace. Miriam had broken the horse's will, and she now regained control of the beautiful animal as he submitted to his master's touch.

Changing the Way We Act

When I took piano lessons, I quickly became frustrated. I didn't want to *learn* how to *play* piano; I wanted to play the piano! Similarly, many times in life we don't want to practice the lesson, but we demand immediate results. When the results don't come instantly, we get frustrated and give up.

Paul said that we become mature "because of practice," and everything mentioned in the previous pages moves us to the desired result of changing the way we act. If we put the cart before the horse and start trying to change our actions without changing our hearts and minds, we will become frustrated. That is what the Pharisees did. It is called legalism, and it does not lead to freedom in Christ or the beautiful life. It leads to bondage and "white washed tombs" that look good on the outside, but are filled with death on the inside. So let's turn our attention now to applying the truths in our minds and hearts to our feet and hands.

Just like Miriam's horse that had a tendency to bolt toward the barn because that was the pattern he had developed after many months, we tend to fall back into old habit patterns. This tendency can only be broken when we are walking by the Spirit and yielding to our Master's touch. But I have to warn you, sometimes you might find yourself going in circles as the Master tries to break your will.

Paul was no stranger to this struggle of changing the way we act. In Romans chapter 7, he lets us have a peek into the battle he faced on a regular basis.

I do not understand what I do. For what I want to do I do not do, but what I hate I do. And if I do what I do not want to do, I agree that the law is good. As it is, it is no longer I myself who do it, but it is sin living in me. I know that nothing good lives in me, that is, in my sinful nature. For I have the desire to do what is good, but I cannot carry it out. For what I do is not the good I want to do; no, the evil I do not want to do—this I keep on doing. Now if I do what I do not want to do, it is no longer I who do it, but it is sin living in me that does it. So I find this law at work: When I want to do good, evil is right there with me. For in my inner being I delight in God's law; but I see another law at work in the members of my body, waging war against the law of my mind and making me a prisoner of the law of sin at work within my members. What a wretched man I am! (vv. 15–24)

Paul was in quite a predicament. He felt wretched. I've been there right along with him. Have you? As long as we depend on our old flesh patterns and old way of doing things, dear sisters, we will feel wretched. Paul knew in his mind what he wanted to do, but his body, like Miriam's strong-willed steed, wanted to do the opposite. Theologians have argued for centuries whether Paul was writing about his life before or after his conversion. I can see arguments for both sides. Although that may remain unclear, one thing is certain—in these verses Paul was a man trying to "do good" in his own strength.

Here's an exercise for you. Go back and reread those verses, marking each time Paul uses the words "I," "my," or "me." How many do you count?

Paul uses at least thirty-two personal pronouns when describing his struggle to make his walk match his talk. That's a lot of "me, myself, and I." Therein lies the problem! When we focus on our own strengths and abilities apart from Christ, we will always come up lacking. We live in a culture that says, "Pull yourself up by your own bootstraps." "If you can dream it, you can achieve it." Hertz Rent-a-Car used to boast, "We try harder." Unfortunately, "we try harder" is the banner flying over many of our churches and hearts today.

I have some startling news for you. Living the Christian life is not difficult—it is impossible, and the harder you try in your own strength, the more frustrated you'll become. Jesus is the only One who has ever lived the perfect Christian life, and He is the only

One who can live it today. The good news is He wants to live it through you!

But how? Paul knew the problem, and he also knew the solution. He was so excited to tell us the answer, he couldn't even wait until Romans 8, but blurted it out at the end of Romans 7: "Who will rescue me from this body of death? Thanks be to God—through Jesus Christ our Lord!" (vv. 24–25).

As Paul discovered, trying harder is not the answer; letting Jesus live through us is. In Galatians 2:20 he said, "I have been crucified with Christ and I no longer live, but Christ lives in me. The life I live in the body, I live by faith in the Son of God, who loved me and gave himself for me." We can never experience freedom walking in the flesh—depending on our own abilities apart from Christ. We only experience freedom walking in the Spirit and identifying with the death, burial, and resurrection of Jesus Christ.

LIFE IN THE SPIRIT

In a factory where delicate fabrics were woven, the machine operators were told to call on the supervisor should the thread at any time become entangled in the equipment. One woman had worked at the factory for many years and knew the machines well. When her threads became entangled in the gears, she tried and tried to pull them out. After several minutes, she had created a disastrous mess, putting the expensive machine in jeopardy. Finally, she called the supervisor and defended herself by saying, "I did my best!"

The supervisor answered, "No, you didn't. To do your best would have been to call on me."

We can try our best to fix ourselves, but doing our best is to call on God and practice holding His hand and walking in the Spirit.

What does the life led by the Spirit look like? Paul paints the stark contrast of the life controlled by the flesh (doing things our way) in Romans 7 with the life controlled by the Spirit (doing things God's way) in Romans 8. The verses in Roman 8 are a balm to the Christian. Here are just a few.

- Therefore, there is now no condemnation for those who are in Christ Jesus (v. 1).
- You received the spirit of sonship. And by him we cry, "Abba, Father" (v. 15).
- We are God's children (v. 16).
- We are co-heirs with Christ (v. 17).
- I consider that our present sufferings are not worth comparing with the glory that will be revealed in us (v. 18).
- In all things God works for the good of those who love him, who have been called according to his purpose (v. 28).
- In all these things we are more than conquerors through him who loved us (v. 37).
- [Nothing] will be able to separate us from the love of God (v. 39).

In Romans 7, when Paul focused on "me, myself, and I," he was pitiful. In Romans 8, when Paul focused on life in the Spirit, he was powerful. This new way of walking is called "sanctification" by theologians. Don't let this word scare you. It simply means "the process of becoming in your behavior what you already are in your identity. Your old self is dead, but the flesh and sin live on, battling your new self daily for control of your life. Spiritual growth and maturity result when you believe the truth about who you are and then do what you are supposed to do to renew your mind and walk in the Spirit."[1]

Walking in the Spirit is characterized by the fruit of the Spirit:

love, joy, peace, patience, kindness, goodness, faithfulness, gentleness, and self-control. Oh how I wish I could reduce life in the Spirit to a formula to follow, but I cannot. Life in the Spirit is the supernatural result of maturing in a personal and ongoing relationship with Jesus Christ. The more intimately we know and obey Him, the more we will become conformed to His image and the more beautiful we will become.

Walking in the Spirit is a consistent moving forward toward the Cross. It is not accomplished by filling up our days with endless activities "working for the Lord." As Jesus told Martha, Mary's industrious sister, He is much more impressed with our sitting at His feet than scurrying around doing "ministry." When we read about the bondage of the Israelites in Exodus 1, we see they were kept under submission of "taskmasters" (NASB). Once again, Satan is not very creative, but very effective. He still has "taskmasters" cracking the whip over our backs today. "Satan knows that he may not be able to stop you from serving God by making you immoral, but he can probably slow you down by simply making you busy."[2]

PITIFUL PATTY OR POWERFUL PAULA

We all agree that we need to live our lives in the Spirit and not in the flesh, but we don't always recognize the flesh when we see it. That is largely because some people's flesh looks better than others.

Let's take Pitiful Patty and Powerful Paula. Pitiful Patty is always depressed, feels like a victim, and tries to get her needs met by being pitiful and whiny. Nothing ever works out for the poor girl. She's learned that if she acts pitiful, people will feel sorry for her and not expect much from her, because she's—well—pitiful, bless her heart.

Then there's Powerful Paula. She takes charge, could run IBM single-handed, and exudes confidence and courage. Powerful Paula gets her needs met by performing well in order to hear those wonderful words, "well done" and "good job." She thrives on the praises of others. People expect a lot from Paula, because she's—well—powerful.

As Christians, Pitiful Patty has an easy time believing 2 Corinthians 12:9, "My strength is made perfect in weakness" (KJV), because she is in tune with her weakness. Paula, on the other hand, resonates with "I can do everything through him who gives me strength" (Philippians 4:13), because she's been doing it on her own all her life anyway.

The truth is, both women need an ultimate makeover. They need to participate in God's exfoliation regimen to slough off dead flesh, get rid of old habits, and start walking in the Spirit, to be conformed to the image of Christ.

Are you a Pitiful Patty or a Powerful Paula? Most of us fall somewhere in between. However, I'll have to admit, most of my life I've tried to make myself look like Powerful Paula while feeling more like Pitiful Patty.

Amazingly, two different children raised in the same household with the same stimuli can form two different flesh patterns or ways of dealing with life. For example, let's take two siblings, Becky and Jonathan. They grew up in a violent home where their parents fought continually. Their father was an alcoholic and their mother was a controller. With this volatile combination, they witnessed many explosive outbursts.

In an attempt to protect their emotions, the two children responded in different ways. Many nights, Becky stood between the two parents, literally breaking up the fights. She became a "fix-it person." Meanwhile, her brother fled the scene and became an "exit person." At first, he got on his bike and pedaled away. Then, when he got older, he grabbed the car keys and drove away.

The two children grew up to be adults with very ingrained patterns of handling stress. Becky continued to be a "fix-it person." She tried to fix everybody and everything. Jonathan continued to be an "exit person," leaving every time life became difficult. He quit the football team in high school when someone questioned his ability. He quit college when the course load became too strenuous. He quit his marriage when he and his wife encountered financial difficulties. He quit ten jobs in ten years because the "bosses were unfair."

Although Becky's unique version of the flesh looks better on the outside, it is flesh nonetheless. Neither will find true peace or happiness until they learn to walk by the Spirit.

Perhaps being a controller (fix-it person) or a quitter (an exit person) is not a flesh pattern to which you can relate. Let me give you another one to chew on. Oh, I hate to admit this, but I fear many sisters will relate—the dents in my armor from fiery arrows attest to it.

Before I became a Christian, I was very "gifted" with a quick, sarcastic wit. Have you ever been in an argument and two hours later thought of a great comeback or slam remark? Not me. I could think of them on the spot. I was good—so good. Why, I could have opened up a side business feeding disgruntled wives, employees, and friends quick comebacks through earphones during confrontations. However, after I accepted Christ as my Savior, it didn't take the Holy Spirit long to convince me that my tongue was not glorifying the Lord. Sure, it brought some laughs, but Jesus wasn't smiling. So I began the arduous task of taming my tongue—which brother James says is next to impossible, by the way.

I memorized Job 40:4, "I put my hand over my mouth," and bit my tongue. It was hard letting all those good sarcastic comments go to waste, but I knew they were only fit for the garbage heap.

That was more than thirty years ago. On many occasions,

when someone tells me about a confrontation with a mother-in-law or a co-worker, my mind still pops up those quick waspish remarks. When a store clerk offers a snide remark, I can usually think of one that's snider. So where's the victory? The victory comes when I choose not to let the words out of my mouth. When I offer blessings instead of cursing. When I put on the humility of Christ and take others' comments without the retribution my tongue would have naturally dished out. That, my friend, is choosing to walk in the Spirit instead of walking in the flesh. It can only happen by the power of the Holy Spirit, and it becomes easier with practice.

How do you begin? You begin just as a baby begins to take those first steps. Victorious days lead to victorious lives. If I were to write a book titled *How to Live the Victorious Christian Life,* it would have two words on every page . . . Follow Jesus. That's it. Obey Him.

When I was praying about a decision that I knew would change my life dramatically, I cried out for the Lord to give me wisdom. Then I read John 2 with fresh eyes and two words jumped out from the pages . . . "Whatever He says to you, *do it*" (v. 5 NASB, italics added). There it is, my friends. That's how you begin. And that's also how you finish well.

There is a good reason this chapter is near the end of the book. We tend to want someone to tell us a magic formula or ten steps to success (or thinner thighs in ten minutes a day). However, understanding the truths in the previous pages makes this chapter possible.

Does a recovering alcoholic never again long for the warm brown liquid to course down her throat and sting her senses? Does the previously promiscuous woman never ponder the thrill of seduction? Does the silenced gossiper never crave the sensation of owning the power of hidden secrets? I am not sure if the desires of the flesh are ever sloughed away for good, but I do know that the more we practice righteousness, the more we follow Him, the more we obey the Master's leading in our lives, the more the glow of the Spirit will shine through us and onto those around us.

chapter 11

A DAY
AT THE SPA:
Spending Time with
the Makeover Artist

I was comfortably snuggled in a warm black leather reclining chair, which vibrated at calibrated intervals. The room was dimly lit with clusters of flickering, scented candles. My mind relaxed as music from stringed instruments wafted through the air like invisible winged fairies. Ahhhh, this was definitely one of my husband's best gifts ever . . . a day at the spa.

I really didn't know what to expect when I walked through the doors to redeem my gift certificate, but I was pleasantly surprised. Betty first dipped my hands into melted paraffin and then placed my wax-coated skin into warmed mittens. She then led me into the candlelit room, seated me in an overstuffed recliner, and told me to relax. She returned after a few moments and exfoliated, massaged, and moisturized my face and scalp. Reluctantly, I then sat up and placed my feet in a warm, bubbly massaging tub. My feet floated on air after the forty-five-minute pulsating bubble bath, calf massage, and pedicure.

Next, my hair submitted to the beautician's comb and brush for a trendy new look. A French manicure made my forty-something hands look young and vibrant. A makeup artist applied the proper colors in all the right places, and I left feeling like a queen.

A day at the spa—what a delightful treat! But that was on a Friday, and by Monday the visit seemed like a distant memory. The dry flakes returned to my face, the tension knots reappeared in my neck, the red polish had chipped around my twin big toes, the bathroom cleaner with bleach had caused my white French manicure to turn a pale shade of yellow, and my hair refused to submit to my commands—exchanging the trendy new look for early American housewife frump.

Yes, every woman loves the idea of spending a day being pampered from head to toe—but the results are temporary and oh-so-fleeting. There is one spa, however, where the results are eternal, the doors are always open, and the makeover artist is always eagerly awaiting our arrival. Every one of God's children has a standing appointment with God, to be refreshed, renewed, and revived today and every day—to be made beautiful with glowing, lasting results.

Everything I've written on previous pages hinges on one pivotal point. In order to experience the ultimate makeover, we must spend time with the Makeover Artist, God. Being conformed to the image of Christ doesn't happen when we merely acquire more head knowledge, memorize more Bible verses, or master Greek and Hebrew derivations and verb tenses. Becoming spiritually beautiful in Christ is a direct result of spending time in His presence, embraced in His love and enveloped in His grace. Moving from one state of glory to the next does not occur by following a list of rules. It is a supernatural result of developing an intimate, ongoing, ever-growing relationship with Jesus Christ. The outward, visible signs of such a relationship occur when we give Jesus total access to our lives. He wants to inhabit every nook and cranny of our minds, wills, and emotions and live His life through us. When He does, our walk will be in tandem with His.

In the New Testament, the Pharisees were the religious experts of their day. They had a lot of head knowledge about God, but had little to no heart relationship with Him. They knew about God, but did not know Him personally. Amazingly, they felt they knew it all, when, in reality, they knew nothing at all.

In the Old Testament, the Israelites were satisfied knowing about God, but never desired to know Him personally. They witnessed miracles He performed and ate food He provided, but remained content partaking of His provisions without ever knowing the Provider.

But Moses was a man who knew God on a personal level. God even referred to Moses as His "friend" (Exodus 33:11; 2 Chronicles 20:7). One defining characteristic of Moses was his frequent trips to God's spa and extended periods of time spent in God's presence. One particular visit lasted for forty days and forty nights (Exodus 24:18). When Moses came home from Mount Sinai, he was radiant—his face actually shone. Moses' visits with God had such glowing results, he had to place a veil over his face so the glory would not blind those who looked at him. In between his times with the Lord, the glorious glow gradually ebbed away (2 Corinthians 3:13). But whenever he spent time in the Lord's presence, he was re-energized and the intensity of the glow returned.

Have you ever had a mountaintop experience during a women's conference, a spiritual retreat, or extended time alone with God? You returned home with a smile on your face, a song in your heart, and a bounce in your step. But after a few days, your husband said something that made the hair stand up on the back of your neck, your teenager broke curfew again, and your neighbor called to complain that your dog dug up her prize rosebush. (I've often said I could be a great Christian if it weren't for people.) It doesn't take much of life to give us a bad case of the *uglies*.

So, how do we maintain that holy glow in our hearts amidst the struggles of daily life? We visit God's spa for the soul on a regular basis. When we do, 2 Corinthians 3:18 becomes a reality in our lives. "And we, who with unveiled faces all reflect the Lord's glory, are being transformed into his likeness with ever-increasing glory, which comes from the Lord, who is the Spirit."

Have you ever noticed how married couples sometimes begin to look alike, speak with similar clichés, and move with mirrored mannerisms? Have you observed lifelong friends use similar words, copy figures of speech, and dovetail ideas? Likewise, when we spend time with God, we will begin to talk like Him, think like Him, and respond to life like Him. Whom do you want to be like? Do you want to be like the women on TV, or do you want to be like Jesus Christ? We will become like the company we keep.

A STANDING APPOINTMENT

I usually visit my hairdresser every six to eight weeks for a trim. However, she has a rather large clientele of older ladies who come once a week—every week. Barbara calls these her "standing" appointments. Unless Esther is on vacation or in the hospital, she has a standing appointment at 10:00 every Tuesday morning. Louise is in the chair every Monday at 12:00 noon, followed by Mabel at 1:00. Each week, Barbara shampoos, curls, cuts, colors (if needed), and sprays their hair. On the days in between, the ladies simply pick, fluff, and reapply spray to keep their sculptured coiffures intact until their next visit. Mayhem breaks loose when Barbara takes a vacation as panic-stricken women scurry about for temporary solutions.

My husband was shocked when I explained this weekly ritual that his own mother had participated in for decades. He couldn't fathom washing his hair only once a week, but I told him churchgoers do a similar thing all the time. They go to church on Sunday for their weekly cleansing and sprucing up and never give God another thought until the following week.

But God has an appointment book with "standing" appointments for each of us—not once a week, but every day. Our names are written in blood, and He is waiting to cleanse us and beautify our souls every morning. To help you remember the importance of this rendezvous with God, I've come up with the simple acrostic DATE. Without keeping a DATE with God on a regular basis, we will not experience the ultimate makeover with lasting results.

D — Determine to Spend Time with God

In my workroom, I have two identical jars. One is three-fourths full of sand, and the other contains fist-sized rocks. The jar of sand represents my activities on any given day: to-do lists, grocery shopping, community projects, housecleaning, etc. The list seems as endless as grains of sand on a beach. The jar containing the large rocks represents what God wants me to do on any given day, which begins by spending time with Him, studying His Word, and praying—my daily beauty treatment.

If I fill the jar with large rocks first, amazingly, I can pour all the sand into the same jar and it fits in nicely around the nooks and crannies. However, if I begin by filling the jar with sand and then try to squeeze the rocks into the same jar, they won't fit.

Likewise, if I start my day spending time with God (the rocks), everything else (the sand) seems to fall into place. If I spring out of bed and hit the floor running to tackle all the tasks that I feel are so necessary for the day first, somehow my time with the Lord just never seems to fit in.

I keep these two jars in my workroom as a reminder to keep my appointment with God each day. This is not a legalistic self-imposed mandate. It is a privilege to have an audience before the King of kings. The jars are there to help remind me that He's waiting for me to show up.

Jesus said to Martha, "Martha, Martha, you are worried and upset about many things, but only one thing is needed. Mary has chosen what is better, and it will not be taken away from her" (Luke 10:41). Mary started her day with the big rocks. Undoubtedly, Martha started hers with sand. The Bible never tells us what Martha and Mary look like, but in my mind's eye, I've always envisioned Martha as harshly stern-faced and Mary as tenderly beautiful. I don't know why—all we're told is one spent time at Jesus' feet and the other spent time in the kitchen. Come to think about it—that's all the reason in the world.

A — Appoint a Specific Time Each Day

Let's face it: We are creatures of habit. If we can establish a specific time to meet with God each day, we will be more likely to show up for our appointment. When Jesus taught His disciples to pray, He said, "Give us this day our daily bread." David and Nehemiah both sought the Lord "day and night," not just when they were in trouble. God provided manna for the Israelites every morning (except on the Sabbath). When a few Israelites tried to gather extra food so they wouldn't have to collect God's provisions the next day, they found their bowls full of worms the next morning. God wants us to seek Him for our daily—not weekly or biannually—bread.

Some tell me that they have their quiet time on the way to

work, in the carpool line, or on their lunch break. This seems to me like going into a five-star restaurant, ordering a multi-course meal, and asking the waiter to put it in a to-go bag.

My best time to visit God's spa is in the morning before the tyranny of the urgent begins to pull on me. When I spend time in the morning, God helps me order my days and keep His perspective on what is happening around me.

In Mark 1:35 (NASB), we see that Jesus also began His days communing with the Father. "In the early morning, while it was still dark, Jesus got up, left the house, and went away to a secluded place, and was praying there." Interestingly, in the next verse, Mark describes a scene where the disciples were frantically looking for Jesus. It seems that the people in the town where Jesus had been the day before were pleading for Him to return and heal some more people. The disciples said, "Everyone is looking for You." And He replied, "Let us go somewhere else to the towns nearby, so that I may preach there also; for that is what I came for" (vv. 37, 38 NASB).

Jesus had met with the Father and received His marching orders for the day. He was able to say yes and no with confidence because He knew what His Father had planned for Him to do on that particular day. Would going back to Capernaum and healing more people have been a good cause? Yes, it would have. But it wasn't what God had planned for Him on that day. He knew how to prioritize the good for the goal.

I don't know about you, but by 8:30 in the morning, my phone is ringing with all kinds of requests and demands on my time. By spending time with God first thing in the morning, I'm able to set my priorities and say yes and no with confidence. In my book *Seven Life Principles for Every Woman*, I mentioned this idea of having a DATE with God each day. I was very reluctant to say that the DATE should be in the morning. I understand the struggles of a mother with a new baby, the woman who works the night shift, or the person who has to leave for a 5:30 A.M. commute to work.

Yes, it *is* more important that you have a quiet time with the Lord than the time you actually have it. However, I'm going to let Bruce Wilkinson tell us his opinion.

> Some Christians I know try to have their meaningful personal times with God just before bed, but I have yet to find a respected spiritual leader throughout history who had devotions at night. Unless you get up early, you're unlikely to break through to a deeper relationship with God. Set aside a significant time and a private place where you can read and write comfortably, think, study, talk to God out loud and weep if you need to. . . . To break through to abiding I must broaden my devoted time—taking it from a morning appointment to an all-day attentiveness to His presence.[1]

The psalmist David wrote, "In the morning, O LORD, you hear my voice; in the morning I lay my requests before you and wait in expectation" (Psalm 5:3).

Studies show that it takes seven weeks of doing something routinely to form a habit. Appoint a specific time each day to spend with the Lord and stick to it for seven weeks. When you've established your "standing" appointment, you will be more likely to show up, and what an incredible life changing habit you will have formed.

T — Take Your Cues from Jesus

When I decided to set up a "standing" appointment with God each day, I wasn't sure exactly what I was supposed to do during that time, so I read to see what Jesus did. First and foremost, I noticed that Jesus spent His time in prayer.

Just the other night, my teenage son was looking for me. The first place he called was my ministry partner's cell phone. He knew the chances were great that I was either with Lysa or she would know where I was. Likewise, when Jesus' disciples were searching for Him in Mark 1:35–37, they knew exactly where to look. He was off with the Father in prayer.

Some of the greatest moments in a Christian's life are a result of spending time in prayer. Jesus spent all night in prayer before He chose His disciples (Luke 6:12). He defeated Satan's temptations after praying and fasting for forty days (Matthew 4:3–11). Prayer preceded His miracles (John 11:41–43) and gave Him the strength to go to the Cross (Luke 22:39–43). Jesus showed us how to have more than a prayer life. He showed us how to have a praying life.

The disciples observed the power that came as Jesus spent time with God in prayer and asked Him to teach them how to pray. He gave them seven simple steps that we have come to know as "the Lord's Prayer." Did the disciples take their cues from Jesus and learn how to pray? Yes, they did! In Acts 2, during their prayer time, the Holy Spirit descended on the disciples and gave them power to spread the gospel through the world. That same Holy Spirit is available to us.

In *Experiencing God*, Henry Blackaby writes, "Prayer is not a substitute for hard work. It is the work!"[2] Prayer isn't meant to change God's mind. It is supposed to align our thinking with God's and to change us with the power necessary to change the world.

Know this, dear sister: Satan knows that *prayerless* lives are *powerless* and *unprotected* lives. He will try to distract you in any way he can. When you sit down to pray, the phone may ring, ten things to add to your to-do lists may mysteriously pop into your mind, your eyelids may become heavy, and the demands and concerns of the day may press in to invade your time—but don't let the Enemy win. Prayer is the makeover tool that turns concerns into comfort, chaos into calm, cowards into conquerors, and worriers into warriors. Keep your appointment in prayer. You'll be amazed how it can be the oil to make the wheels of the day turn smoothly.

E — Equip Yourself for Every Good Work

If you ran out to your mailbox and retrieved four pieces of mail—a letter from Aunt Susie, a bill from the phone company, a department store flyer, and a letter from God—which one would you open first? I don't know about you, but I'd rip open that letter from God faster than a two-year-old tearing into a beautifully wrapped Christmas present! The truth is, God has sent us a wonderful love letter, filled with incredible treasures, words of endearment, instruction to equip us for life, and makeover tips to make us beautiful from the inside out. All we have to do is open the pages of the Bible.

Matthew Henry said prayer is a letter we send to God; the Bible is a letter God has sent to us.[3] God has given us the Bible to communicate with us. We come to know God better through what the Bible reveals about Him, and, through that revelation, He releases His power in our lives.

Second Timothy 3:16–17 (NASB) says, "All Scripture is inspired by God and profitable for teaching, for reproof, for correction, for training in righteousness; so that the man of God may be adequate, equipped for every good work." When you read God's Word and hide it in your heart, you are equipping yourself for the days ahead. I love how 1 Peter 1:13 says, "Therefore, *gird* your minds for action" (NASB 1977 edition). When I see the word *gird* I can't help but think of my grandmother's old-fashioned girdle. It held her in, held her up, and she wouldn't leave home without it. Likewise, we shouldn't leave home without girding our minds for action!

When I am under stress, I tend to have three reccurring dreams. In one, I'm in high school, and it's the day of final exams, but I realize I haven't gone to that class all year. In my second dream,

I'm working as a dental hygienist with one patient in the chair and five patients in the waiting room. I'm two hours behind and can't find my instruments. In my third dream, I'm standing behind a podium in a crowded room. I'm not dressed in a power suit but in my birthday suit. After some consideration, I realize that each of these bad dreams is about not being equipped—not being prepared.

The Bible is designed to lead us to God and draw us into a closer walk with Him. As we walk closer to Him, we will experience His power in our lives. He performs a makeover and turns defeat, discouragement, despair, doubt, dread, and depression into love, joy, peace, patience, kindness, goodness, faithfulness, gentleness, and self-control.

A. W. Tozer once said:

> Every farmer knows the hunger of the wilderness. The hunger which no modern farm machinery, no improved agricultural methods can quite destroy no matter how well prepared the soil, how well-kept the fences, how carefully painted the buildings, let the owner neglect for a while his prized and valued acres and they will revert again to the wilds and be swallowed by the jungle or wasteland. The bias of nature is toward the wilderness, never toward the fruitful field.

If we desire to cultivate the fruit of the Spirit in our lives, we cannot leave our spiritual lives to chance but must nuture our relationship with Christ.

GETTING STARTED

If you are not in the habit of spending time with God each day, I want to encourage you to start with realistic goals. Begin with spending five minutes a day—three minutes reading the Bible and two minutes praying. Then increase your time to fifteen minutes a day—perhaps seven minutes reading the Bible and eight minutes praying. If having a quiet time with the Lord each day is a new concept for you, deciding to set aside an hour each day may be inviting failure. Start slowly. Just as a person who has not been eating due to illness must start by eating small bits at a time, you may need to begin by taking small bits of the Word of God. Once you begin to feast on God's Word and bask in His presence, the benefits and beauty that follows will be all the enticement you need to visit God's spa and be continually transformed into the image of Christ.

Perhaps you've tried many times to begin having quiet times with God each day, but have broken your appointment. Please don't become discouraged. "Come near to God and he will come near to you" (James 4:8). When one of the greatest men in the Bible, Peter, didn't show up for Jesus and denied Him three times just before His crucifixion, Jesus didn't reprimand or scold him. He simply asked Peter to reaffirm his love (see John 21:15-17). "Peter, do you love Me?" He asked.

That's what He's saying to you. "Daughter, do you love Me?" "Call to me and I will answer you and tell you great and unsearchable things you do not know" (Jeremiah 33:3). "'Return to me,' declares the LORD Almighty, 'and I will return to you'" (Zechariah 1:3).

chapter 12

MY PERSONAL JOURNEY:

Putting the Pieces Together

I had been speaking all morning at a ladies' retreat in Virginia and welcomed the one-hour lunch break to rest my feet and my voice. Lisa, the women's director, was very attentive and sat with me while I munched on salad and sipped sweet iced tea. She was a beautiful woman with stylish short blonde hair, a winning vibrant smile, and a bubbly personality that spilled over with Jesus Christ. Her crisp blue suit accentuated the aquamarine of her eyes, and her matching shoes put the finishing touches on a woman who looked like she "had it all together." It was very evident by the hugs and pats on the back that Lisa was the spiritual mentor and confidant to many women in the church.

Nonchalantly, I asked, "Lisa, what's your story? How did you come to Christ?"

I can tell you, there is no way I could have ever been

prepared for what I heard over the next thirty minutes. Brace yourself and listen to her story.

LISA'S MAKEOVER

"Sharon, I was born into a family with three older brothers. I don't remember much of my early years, but one of my earliest childhood memories is when I was five years old standing over a bridge and thinking, *If I fell over this bridge into the river and disappeared, no one would ever care.* I always felt like something was wrong with me—like I was a misfit or an irregular.

"I remember my mother saying to me, 'What's wrong with you?'

"As a little girl, I thought—*I don't know, but I know it must be something!* I felt uncomfortable in my own skin—like I didn't belong, wasn't accepted, lovable, or valuable.

"When I was thirteen, I took my first drink of wine. I actually downed three bottles in one sitting. It felt good. I felt good. All my insecurities were gone. I lost my virginity when I was fourteen and smoked marijuana for the first time that same year. For the next twenty-eight years, I chased after anything and everything to numb my pain. Whether it was food, exercise, shopping, men, alcohol, or drugs—I sought after anything that would transport me into a different world for a while and fill the gaping void in my soul.

"After high school, I worked in Washington, D.C., at a law firm. But that didn't last very long, as I was fired for falsifying records. After that, I went to work as a bartender. My alcohol and drug use began to climb, and I began to plummet. I moved in with a man who beat me up on a regular basis. I felt I deserved it.

"One night, I reached the end of my rope and tried to kill myself with sleeping pills. For some reason, I called my mom to say good-bye, and she alerted the rescue squad. Even though I spent time in the psychiatric ward, I left the hospital just as lost and confused and desperate as when the ambulance had brought me in.

"Cocaine is very expensive, and I needed a way to support my habit, so I became a prostitute on the streets of Washington, D.C. With every trick, a piece of me died. Pretty soon, I became numb to it all. Amazingly, I was arrested, not for prostitution, but for writing bad checks. My attorney got me out of jail and into a recovery program. This was the beginning of a long road to recovery, but the reason I am alive today is because I met someone. It wasn't a lawyer, a mentor, or the man of my dreams. His name is Jesus Christ, and He's the one who set me free."

I sat there with a lump in my throat, tears in my eyes, and love for my Savior pounding in my heart. I had asked a simple question, "Tell me your story." Never had I had such a filling, delicious lunch in all my life.

What exactly happened to Lisa? How did God transform an alcoholic, cocaine-addicted prostitute into a pure, holy, lovely Christian woman who is so filled with the Holy Spirit it seeps out and spills on to everyone she comes in contact with? Lisa met the Makeover artist and experienced the ultimate makeover—change from the inside out. She will be the first to tell you it has been a long process, but worth every trial, struggle, victory, and celebration along the way. Let me take a moment now to put some of the pieces of this book together and tell you my story.

MY PERSONAL MAKEOVER

By nature, I am a very organized person. Most days run fairly smoothly. My files are color coded, my spices are alphabetized, and I've only lost my car keys twice in my life. Someone approached me about writing a book on organization to help women find order amongst the chaos, but in truth, I don't really know what I do. It is just the way I came out of the womb. I probably began organizing the doctor's surgical instruments and straightening his face mask the moment he cut the cord and popped me on the bottom.

We tend to learn through the struggles and trials of life, not through what comes easily. I can assure you that is how I learned about experiencing the ultimate makeover—through the Refiner's fire. I have lived every page of this book. I have given you many pieces of the makeover puzzle in the preceding pages. Now, I would like to fit those pieces together so you can get the entire picture in one life story. The best way I know to do that is to take you down my own personal road to the ultimate makeover.

Like many children living through the Depression in rural North Carolina, my parents graduated from high school, got married a few days later, and had a baby ten months following. Four years after my brother was born, I came on the scene. From the very beginning, my parents had a rocky marriage. I don't remember much about the first five years of my life, but I do remember many heated arguments and violent outbursts. I felt as though I lived on an earthquake fault line, never knowing when the big one was going to hit.

My father was a successful businessman who spent many hours away from home. We lived in a beautiful brick ranch home with ninety-foot pine trees forming a shady canopy over our roof. With two kids and a collie named Lassie, we looked like the typical all-American family. But behind the peaceful exterior loomed a deep, dark secret.

My father had a drinking problem and many nights came home in violent fits of rage. My parents fought both verbally and physically in my presence, and I saw many things that a little child

◆ ◆

should never see and heard words that a little child should never hear. As a child I remember going to bed, pulling the covers up tightly under my chin and praying that I could hurry up and go to sleep to shut out the sound of my parents yelling and fighting. On several occasions, I awoke to broken furniture, my mother's black eye, and a weeping father making promises that it would never happen again.

As a little girl, even though people said I was very cute, I never felt pretty or acceptable. I longed to be cherished or valued, but felt I was always in the way and a poor excuse for a daughter. My parents did love me, but they were so wrapped up in their own struggles they didn't always know how to show it.

I want to make something very clear here. Yes, my parents made many mistakes, but they were not the real enemy. Satan was. He used the struggles of my mother, born a middle child of twelve during the Depression, and the struggles of my father, the youngest of six children whose father died when he was five years old, during that same time in history, to perpetuate a cycle of inferiority, insecurity, and inadequacy. They did the best they could with what they had.

In the first grade, I had trouble with spelling and spent the first year of the spelling train in the caboose, where you went when you misspelled a word. My feeling that I was not very bright was confirmed in my mind when I had to wear a name tag for two weeks with the word *the* taped to my chest to teach me never to miss that word again. By the time I was six years old, I learned how to spell the word *the,* but that's not all I learned about myself. I learned that I was stupid.

As a child, I felt lost and alone. Inferiority, insecurity, and inadequacy became the grid system, the filter, formed over my mind. By the time I was a teenager, that filter was stitched firmly in place, and every thought I had, every experience I interpreted, had to go through that negative grid system. If you had seen me as a teenager, the grades that I made (National Honor Society), the clubs I was involved in (cheerleader for six years), the boyfriends I had, and the designer clothes I wore, you would have never known that I felt that way about myself or was in that type of bondage. You can never tell the pain on the inside by the appearance of the outside. I was like the quote, "Many times under silken apparel lives a threadbare soul."

But God didn't leave me in my ugly state. When I was twelve years old, I became friends with a girl in my neighborhood, Wanda Henderson. Her mother took me under her wing and loved me like I was her own child. Mrs. Henderson knew what was going on in my home, and she knew about my broken heart. I loved being at the Hendersons' home. Mr. and Mrs. Henderson hugged and kissed each other in front of us and even had pet names for each other. I had never seen married people act like this before, and it was a breath of fresh air. I didn't know why that family was so different from mine, but I knew that difference had something to do with Jesus Christ.

Amazingly, my family, with all our struggles, were members of a church. Yes, with all the alcohol and fighting, we went to a very politically correct, socially prestigious church—fighting all the way to the front door. Eventually, Mrs. Henderson invited me to go to church with them. The Hendersons' church was different. They talked about having a personal relationship with Jesus Christ, something I had never heard before. I went to this church and drank in every word the pastor and teachers had to say about a Savior who loved me so much He gave His life for me on Calvary's cross so that I could have eternal life.

The following year, Mrs. Henderson started a Bible study for teenagers in the neighborhood, and I began a love affair with God's Word. One night, when I was fourteen, Mrs. Henderson asked me if I was ready to accept Jesus as Lord of my life. I said yes, and the makeover began. I received a new, living spirit when I was "born again," but the process of being conformed to the image of Christ, the ultimate makeover, was in its infancy. Every verse about my new identity, who I am, what I have, and where I am in Christ became mine; however, I never knew the promises existed.

At first, my parents were leery of my "newfound religion," but my love for the Lord was hard to resist or deny. Two years after I gave my life to Jesus, my mother accepted Him as her personal Savior. Then three years later, through a series of events, twists, and turns that only our heavenly Father could orchestrate, my earthly father gave his life to Christ. In a matter of six years, God had worked an incredible miracle in the life of my family.

But what about those feelings of inferiority, inadequacy, and insecurity that had been burned into my mind? Did they go away the moment I became a Christian? No, they did not. As I mentioned before, I didn't even know they were there. I have already told you how God led me down the road to forgiveness. I had to learn to put the past behind me and move forward. This wasn't an easy task, but I can honestly say I was stuck in the quagmire of the past, unable to move forward spiritually, until I put it behind me.

FURTHER STEPS IN THE MAKEOVER

From the time I was fourteen until I was in my early thirties, I always felt like there was something wrong with me spiritually—like I had walked into a movie twenty minutes late and had to spend the entire time trying to figure out what was going on. I wondered why I struggled so much to live the victorious Christian life. I had a wonderful husband and a great child, taught Bible studies at a scripturally solid church, and surrounded myself with strong Christian friends. But something was missing—I didn't know who I was.

Then one day, I picked up a book by Dr. Neil Anderson, *Victory over the Darkness*, and read a list of who I was in Christ. The door to understanding my new identity flew wide open. For the next ten years, I spent many hours in God's spa learning the truths of who I am, what I have, and where I am in Christ. I went back to the Enemy's camp and took what he stole from me. No longer would I be that little girl in the first grade sitting in the caboose of the spelling train who thought she was stupid or that scared child who thought nobody loved her. They were lies—all lies. I had the mind of Christ and had everything I needed for life and godliness. It has been a tedious process to remove that old grid system stitch by stitch, but God has been the one holding the needle, and all He's asked me to do is stand still while He picks them out.

I can write about having a confidence makeover because I've seen how God took an insecure girl like me and transformed her into someone who knows what God can do through a life totally yielded to Him. I can write about having a faith-lift because I have seen the difference it makes when we believe and act like God tells the truth. I can write about the battle for the mind and changing the way we think because I have fought (and still fight) the Enemy's lies on a daily basis. I can write about leaving the past behind because I've left much baggage by the roadside and cast it at Jesus' feet, never to return to pick it up again. I can write about a change of wardrobe because I sat for many years in desperation and shame with Tamar, but rejoiced when I finally accepted the mantle of a princess from my Redeemer. I can write about exfoliating bits and pieces of old habits and thought patterns because I'm still in the process of sloughing them off every day.

Oh dear sister, I long to be with you right now. This book is so much a part of my life. It isn't my first book, but without the story of the ultimate makeover, there would have never been any of the ones before it or the ones that will follow. How I have longed to grab your hand and take you to God's spa to experience the ultimate makeover. Thank you for joining me. I can already tell, the glory of Christ is radiating from your face as you reflect His glory. You are beautiful, dear one. Absolutely radiant.

NOTES

Chapter 1: A Makeover, Please!

1. "Beauty Contest" by Carla Muir. Used by permission.

2. Plastic Surgery Information Service www.plasticsurgery.org/mediactr/2000release.htm

3. Mimi Avins, "Teens Invest Heavily to Look Good," The Santa Rosa, California Press Democrat, 3 July 2001, D1.

Chapter 2: Spiritual Makeover

1. Charles Swindoll, The Tale of the Tardy Oxcart (Nashville: Word, 1998), 500.

2. Jack Odell, in Lloyd Cory, Quote Unquote (ChariotVictor, 1977); quoted in Charles R. Swindoll, The Tale of the Tardy Ox Cart (Nashville: Word, 1998), 503.

3. Neil Anderson and other writers have come up with similar lists of the Christian's identity.

4. Neil Anderson, Victory over the Darkness (Ventura, Calif.: Regal, 1990), 37.

Chapter 3: Mirror, Mirror on the Wall

1. NIV Study Bible, General Editor, Kenneth Barker (Grand Rapids: Zondervan, 1995), 895.

2. Neil Anderson, Living Free in Christ (Ventura, Calif.: Regal, 1993), 72.

3. Robert J. Morgan, *Nelson's Complete Book of Stories, Illustrations, and Quotes* (Nashville: Nelson, 2000), 46.

4. Anabel Gilham, *The Confident Woman* (Eugene, Oreg.: Harvest House, 1993), 111–12.

Chapter 4: Confidence Makeover

1. Thomas Watson, *Gleanings from Thomas Watson* (Morgan, Pa.: Soli Deo Gloria, 1995), 49.

2. Barbara Graham, "Shortcuts to Confidence," *Self,* July 1997:116.

3. Susie Fields, "Super Confidence and How to Get It," *Salon Ovations,* September 1996:30.

4. W. E. Vine, Merrill F. Unger, William White Jr., *Vine's Expository Dictionary of Old and New Testament Words* (Nashville: Nelson, 1985), 1.

5. Neil Anderson, *Living Free in Christ* (Ventura, Calif.: Regal, 1993), 70.

Chapter 5: Faith-Lift

1. Kenneth L. Barker and John R. Kohlenberger III, *Zondervan NIV Bible Commentary, Volume 2: New Testament* (Grand Rapids: Zondervan, 1994), 992.

2. A. W. Tozer, *The Best of Tozer* (Grand Rapids: Baker, 1978), 120.

3. Oswald Chambers, *My Utmost for His Highest* (Grand Rapids: Discovery House, 1992), May 30.

4. ©1998 Integrity's Hosanna! Music/ASCAP c/o Integrity Incorporated, 1000 Cody Road, Mobile, AL 36695. Used by permission.

5. NIV Study Bible, General Editor, Kenneth Barker (Grand Rapids: Zondervan, 1995), 1464.

6. "Trust His Heart," Eddie Carswell/Babbie Mason, Causing Change Music (Admin. by Dayspring Music, Inc.), Dayspring Music, Inc., May Sun Music (Admin. by Word Music, Inc.), Word Music, Inc. All rights reserved. Used by permission.

7. Chambers, *My Utmost for His Highest,* June 5.

Chapter 6: Mind Makeover

1. NIV Study Bible, General Editor, Kenneth Barker (Grand Rapids: Zondervan, 1995), 12.

2. Beth Moore, *Breaking Free* (Nashville: LifeWay, 1999), 184.

3. Ibid., 194.

4. Neil Anderson, *The Bondage Breaker* (Eugene, Oreg.: Harvest House, 1990), 23.

5. Annabel Gillham, *The Confident Woman* (Eugene, Oreg.: Harvest House, 1993), 97.

Chapter 7: Exercise Regimen

1. Jean Lush, *Women and Stress* (Grand Rapids: Revell, 1992), 113.

2. Kenneth L. Barker and John R. Kohlenberger III, *NIV Commentary* (Grand Rapids: Zondervan, 1994), 806.

3. Spiros Zodhiates, et al., eds., *The Complete Word Study Dictionary: New Testament* (Chattanooga, Tenn.: AMG Publishers, 1992), 229.

* *

4. Beth Moore, *Living Beyond Yourself* (Nashville: LifeWay, 1998), 120.

5. Philip Yancey, *What's So Amazing About Grace?* (Grand Rapids: Zondervan, 1997), 90.

6. Corrie ten Boom, *Tramp for the Lord* (Grand Rapids: Revell, 1974), 83–86.

7. Ibid., 83.

8. Beth Moore, *Breaking Free* (Nashville: LifeWay, 1999), 75.

9. Carole Mayhall, *Lord Teach Me Wisdom* (Colorado Springs: NavPress, 1979), 155.

10. Quote magazine, July 1991; quoted in *The Tale of the Tardy Ox Cart* (Nashville: Word, 1998), 210.

Chapter 8: The Weight Loss Program

1. C. S. Lewis, *Mere Christianity* (Nashville: Broadman and Holman, 1996), 104.

2. Henry Blackaby and Richard Blackaby, *Experiencing God Day-by-Day* (Nashville: Broadman and Holman, 1997), 193.

3. Malcolm Smith, *Forgiveness* (Tulsa, Okla.: Pillar, 1992), 6–7.

4. Charles R. Swindoll, *Joseph: From Pit to Pinnacle, Bible Study Guide* (Dallas: Word, 1984), i.

5. Beth Moore, *Breaking Free* (Nashville: LifeWay, 1999), 84.

6. Ibid., 5.

7. Neil Anderson, *Victory over the Darkness* (Ventura, Calif.: Regal, 1990), 204.

8. F. B. Meyer, *Devotional Commentary of Philippians* (Grand Rapids: Kregel, 1979), 183–84.

Chapter 9: A Brand New Wardrobe

1. James Strong, from the *Hebrew and Chaldee Dictionary of Exhaustive Concordance of the Bible* (Nashville: Holman Bible Publishers, n.d.), 58.

Chapter 10: Exfoliate the Old

1. Neil Anderson, *Victory over the Darkness* (Ventura, Calif.: Regal, 1990), 85.

2. Ibid., 102.

Chapter 11: A Day at the Spa

1. Bruce Wilkinson, *Secrets of the Vine* (Sisters, Oreg.: Multnomah, 2001), 107, 109.

2. Henry Blackaby and Richard Blackaby, *Experiencing God Devotional* (Nashville: Broadman and Holman, 1997), 276.

3. John Blanchard, comp., *Gathered Gold* (Durham, England: Evangelical Press, 1984), 14.

DEEP CLEANSING—
Bible Study

LESSON ONE

1. Read Genesis 1:24-28; 2:7 and note the difference between how God created animals and man. What made man unique?

2. Read Genesis 2:17 and note the penalty for eating of the Tree of Knowledge of Good and Evil.

3. How did sin enter the world? Through whom? (Romans 5:12-19)

4. What does Ephesians 2:1 say about our state before we accept Christ?

5. Read Matthew 23:27–28. How is a spiritually dead person who acts "religious" like a *whitewashed tomb*?

6. How is spiritual life made available? Through whom? (Romans 5:12–19)

7. If you had been with Nicodemus the night Jesus told him "You must be born again," how would you explain what Jesus meant? (John 3:3)

8. How did Paul see himself as a "born again" believer? (2 Corinthians 5:17)

9. Read and record what Jesus said about "life."
   a. John 1:4
   b. John 6:33, 35
   c. John 11:25
   d. John 14:6
   e. 1 John 5:12

LESSON TWO

1. Read Ephesians 2:1–3 and list everything you learn about the state of a person before the person accepts Christ.

2. The book of Romans wonderfully outlines the spiritual makeover that happens when each person accepts Jesus Christ as Lord and Savior. Look up and record the following verses.
   a. Romans 3:23
   b. Romans 6:23
   c. Romans 5:8
   d. Romans 10:9–10

e. Romans 10:13

f. Romans 8:1

3. Two of my favorite words in the Bible are found in Romans 5:8: "but God." Do you have a "but God" situation in your life? Do you recall a situation that seemed hopeless at the time, "but God" intervened? Take a moment and record the situation briefly.

4. Salvation is a powerful word that can be broken down into past, present, and future. Yes, salvation happens the moment we accept Christ, but there is more to come. In Genesis 1, the writer tells us that God created time. Before there was morning and evening, there was no such thing as time. While we are time creatures, God is not. He sees all of eternity at once. We see it minute by minute. Let's look at salvation in the perspective of time. Match the following explanations with the correct word.

a. We have been saved from the penalty of sin.

(1) Glorification (2 Thessalonians 1:10)

b. We are being saved from the power of sin.

(2) Sanctification (1 Thessalonians 4:3–7)

c. We will be saved from the presence of sin.

(3) Justification (Romans 4:25)

Now let's do the exercise again, focusing on the time frame of each.

a. We have been saved from the penalty of sin.

(1) past

b. We are being saved from the power of sin.

(2) future

c. We will be saved from the presence of sin.

(3) present

5. How does knowing that God sees past, present, and future all at once help you understand Ephesians 2:4–6?

LESSON THREE

1. Now that you know who you are in Christ, let's look at a few more verses about what comes with our new identity.
   a. Ephesians 1:4
   b. Ephesians 1:7–8
   c. Ephesians 2:4–5
   d. Ephesians 2:18
   e. Ephesians 3:12
   f. Colossians 1:14
   g. Colossians 1:27
   h. Colossians 2:7
   i. Colossians 2:10
   j. Colossians 2:12
   k. Colossians 2:13
   l. Colossians 3:1–4

2. Read the following and look at what Christ endured to make our new identity possible.
   a. Isaiah 53
   b. Hebrews 2:6–10
   c. 2 Corinthians 5:21

3. Read Isaiah 43:1–10 and answer the following.
   a. According to Isaiah 43:10, why were we chosen by God?
   b. What is the difference between "to know" and "to believe"?
   c. How does God feel about you?
   d. Why were you created?

4. Read 2 Corinthians 3 and note everything you see about the word *glory.*

5. If you could describe what glory "looks like," what would you say? Use your imagination. There is no right or wrong answer here.

6. What did Jesus show us while He was here on earth? (Hebrews 1:3)

7. What do we show the world by our lives?

8. What does Paul call Christians in 2 Corinthians 3:2? Who is "reading" you?

LESSON FOUR

1. Read Exodus 3:10–4:17. Make two columns on your paper. In one column note Moses' objections to God's call on his life, and in the other note God's responses to those fears or objections.

2. Read Joshua 1:5–9.
   a. What was God's commission to Joshua?
   b. What were God's specific promises to Joshua?

3. Thought question: Why did Noah continue building the ark even though he had never seen rain and the townspeople made fun of him (Genesis 6)? How does this relate to confidence? What was the result of his obedience?

4. Where does fear originate? (2 Timothy 1:7)

5. One of the seeds of fear is dependence on our own abilities. Read 2 Corinthians 1:9 and note what Paul said was the purpose of hardships.

6. Read the following and note what you learn about the importance of depending on Christ in us instead of on our own abilities and talents.
   a. 2 Corinthians 3:5
   b. 2 Corinthians 4:7
   c. Philippians 2:13
   d. Philippians 3:3

7. Read and record Philippians 4:13.
   a. Where was Paul when he wrote this verse? (Philippians 1:13)
   b. What were his living conditions?
   c. Do you think he became discouraged at times?
   d. How would you feel if God called you into ministry, but you ended up in prison?
   e. With this in mind, what can you conclude about what Paul means by "all things"?

8. Now go back and read all of Philippians 4, and note every reason for Paul's confidence.

9. What is the hope of 1 Thessalonians 5:24?

LESSON FIVE

1. Read 2 Timothy 4:7 and describe faith as a noun (object).

2. Read James 2:17–18 and describe faith as a verb (action).

3. In regard to your ultimate makeover, read Hebrews 11:1, and write it out in your own words.

4. Where does faith come from? (Ephesians 2:8–9)

5. Why do you think we cannot please God without faith? (Hebrews 11:6)

6. Read the following and note: Faith is essential for _____.
   a. Ephesians 3:17
   b. Ephesians 3:12
   c. Ephesians 2:8–9
   d. 1 Timothy 1:12; 2 Timothy 2:2
   e. 1 Corinthians 4:12

7. One reason we have little faith in people is that they change their minds and many times do not do what they promise. Look at Hebrews 13:8 and note how God is different from people.

8. All of us have bouts with doubts. Let's take a few minutes and focus on someone very close to Jesus who had questions of his own.
   a. Read Luke 1:39–44. What did the unborn child, John the Baptist, do when Mary walked into his mother's home?
   b. Read John 1:29–34. What did John call Jesus? What did he hear God say? (See the parallel passage, Luke 3:22.)
   c. How long had John known that Jesus was the Messiah? (Hint: Look back at a.)
   d. Read Luke 7:18–28. Where was John at this time? (Mark 6:17–18)
   e. Why was he there?
   f. What were his disciples telling him?

g. What did he ask them to do?

h. What do you think caused John to doubt or question if Jesus was the Messiah, even though we have evidence that he had believed it before anyone else?

9. Sometimes our circumstances cause us to doubt God. Let's look at one final passage to see how God's timing is perfect. Read John 11:1–44.

a. How did Jesus feel about Lazarus?

b. What happened while Jesus waited before He went to Lazarus?

c. How long had Lazarus been in the tomb by the time Jesus arrived?

d. Was Jesus late?

e. What was His reason for waiting?

f. What insight does this give you as to why God does not always answer our prayers in our time frame?

g. Is He ever late? (Romans 5:6)

LESSON SIX

1. Read Isaiah 26:3–6. Whom will God keep in perfect peace?

2. Read Romans 8:5–8 and record everything you learn about the mind that thinks according to the Spirit and the mind that thinks according to the flesh.

3. On what are we to "set our minds"? (Colossians 3:2)

4. What part do you think prayer plays in setting your mind on things above? (Philippians 4:6–7)

5. Read Philippians 4:8 and make a list of what we are to think about. Beside each entry, write a word that represents the opposite thought. On a scale of one to ten, with ten being the positive thoughts and zero being the negative thoughts, how would you judge your thinking?

6. Read Isaiah 50:5–9. What do you think Isaiah meant by "set my face like flint"?

7. What did Jesus say was the most important commandment? (Matthew 22:37)
   Why is loving God with your entire mind so important?

8. What does King David pray regarding his mind? (Psalm 26:2)

LESSON SEVEN

Paul tells us not to be ignorant of Satan's schemes. In order to do this, I believe we need to spend a little time understanding exactly whom we are fighting.

1. Read Genesis 3:13–15. What is Satan's fate?

2. Now that you've looked at the first book of the Bible, flip over to the last. Read Revelation 12:9. What parallel do you see between this verse and Genesis 3:13–15?

3. Read Ezekiel 28:11–19 and list everything you learn about the king of Tyre. This passage is often thought to refer to Satan. What do you see to support this theory?

4. How does John describe Satan in John 8:44? How can this help you take every thought captive?

5. How did Satan influence Ananias in Acts 5:3?

6. Read 1 Peter 5:6–11.
   a. What is Satan doing now?
   b. What are we told to do?
   c. What will God do?

7. What is Satan's strategy? (2 Corinthians 11:12–15)

8. Read 1 Timothy 4:1–3 and note why it is so important to know the truth in these last days.

9. What did Jesus come to do? (1 John 3:8)

10. Read Luke 11:14–26 and answer the following questions.
    a. Who is the strong man?
    b. Who is the stronger man?
    c. What will the stronger man do to the strong man's arsenal?
    d. What will the stronger man do with the spoil?
    e. What is a way to have a "no vacancy" sign if Satan were to return to oppress someone? (Ephesians 5:18)
    f. Read and rejoice over 1 John 4:4.

LESSON EIGHT

1. Read the following and note what the verses say about forgiveness of our sins:
   a. Hebrews 10:10, 14–22
   b. Isaiah 43:25
   c. Romans 5:1

2. If we do not believe that God has forgiven us, what does that say about our faith?

3. Why did the Israelites not enter the Promised Land? (Hebrews 3:18–19)

4. What might you not be receiving that God wants to give you, because of your unbelief? If you do not believe God has forgiven you, what "promised land" might you not be able to enter this side of heaven?

5. Skim 2 Samuel 11 and 12.
    a. What was the result of David's sin?
    b. David wrote Psalm 51 during this time in his life. What can you glean about the attitude of true repentance from this psalm?
    c. Even though David had committed a terrible sin, how did the author of 1 Samuel describe him? (1 Samuel 13:14)

6. Read John 8:1–11.
    a. What did Jesus say *about* the woman caught in adultery?
    b. What did Jesus say *to* the woman caught in adultery?

7. How did the sinful woman in Luke 7:36–50 feel about Jesus?

8. Many who struggle to accept God's forgiveness feel unclean even though the Bible proclaims that they are clean (Romans 8:1). This reminds me of the salutation people with leprosy had to make when they approached another person. They shouted, "Unclean! Unclean!" In the story of the ten lepers recorded in Luke 17:11–19, when did their healing actually take place? (v. 14).

9. Naaman was an army commander who had leprosy. Read his story in 2 Kings 5:1–19 and answer the following questions.

   a. What did Elisha tell him to do?

   b. What was Naaman's initial reaction to these instructions?

   c. How did his men convince him to obey?

   d. What was the result of his obedience?

   e. Have you ever felt that God's offer for forgiveness of your sins was too simple to believe? Have you ever felt if it were more dramatic or severe, your forgiveness would be more believable?

   f. What is the result of your obedience to accept God's solution to become clean?

   g. What were Elijah's final words to Naaman? (v. 19)

LESSON NINE

1. Read each verse and note the attire of each person Satan attacked.

   a. Luke 8:26–33

   b. Acts 19:13–16

   c. Mark 14:52

2. While Satan desires to expose our shame, God desires to cover it. Read Zechariah 3:1–5 and note Joshua's change of wardrobe.

3. Look up the following verses and note what they say about our new wardrobe.

   a. Psalm 30:11

   b. Isaiah 61:10

   c. Galatians 3:26–27

   d. Romans 13:14

   e. Colossians 3:12

4. Let's take some time and focus on that last verse, Colossians 3:12. Here Paul says we are to be clothed in humility. The opposite of humility is pride. Look up the word *pride* in the dictionary and record the definition.

   a. Read Proverbs 6:16–19 and note the seven things the Lord finds detestable. What kind of eyes does the Lord hate, according to Proverbs 6:17?

   b. How was Satan prideful before he was cast out of heaven? (Ezekiel 28:2) What was the origin of Satan's sin?

   c. How did Satan tempt Eve with pride? (Genesis 3:5) What was the root of Adam and Eve's sin?

   d. What happens when God's people are arrogant and don't give glory to God? (Jeremiah 13:15–17)

5. What do the following verses say about pride?

   a. Proverbs 8:13

   b. Proverbs 11:2

   c. Proverbs 13:10

   d. Proverbs 16:18

   e. Obadiah 1:3

   f. James 4:6, 10

6. What is God able to do to the proud? (Daniel 4:37)

7. The opposite of pride is humility. Look up and define *humility*.

8. Read Philippians 2:5–11 and describe the perfect picture of humility.

9. We are told to clothe ourselves with humility. In light of Philippians 2:5–11, what might that look like for us?

LESSON TEN

1. Read Galatians 5:17. How well do the Spirit and the flesh work together?

2. Read Galatians 5:19–21 and Ephesians 5:3–5 and list some visible characteristics of walking in the flesh.

3. Read Galatians 5:22 and note some visible characteristics of walking in the Spirit.

4. Which is the greatest fruit of the Spirit? (1 Corinthians 13:13)

5. If we passed each action through a filter of love, which characteristics of the flesh noted in question #2 would be eliminated?

6. What is one of the greatest signs of maturity among believers? (1 John 5:3)

7. When are we most like God? (1 John 4:16–17)

8. When are others most likely to see God in us? (1 John 4:12)

9. Would you say love is an action or an emotion?

10. How do we become mature? (Hebrews 5:11–14)

11. A big factor in overcoming the flesh and changing the way we act is by overcoming temptation. Look up the following verses and note what you learn about temptation.

a. Why is Jesus able to help us when we are tempted? (Hebrews 2:17–18)

b. How can He sympathize with our weaknesses? (Hebrews 4:15)

c. How did Jesus instruct us to pray about temptation? (Matthew 6:13)

d. Who is actually doing the tempting? (James 1:13–14; Luke 4:1–13)

e. What does God promise to provide in the midst of each temptation? (1 Corinthians 10:13)

LESSON ELEVEN

1. Read the following verses and notice what Jesus was doing. Also note what was going on beforehand.
   a. Luke 6:12
   b. Luke 9:28
   c. Matthew 14:23
   d. Matthew 26:36
   e. Mark 6:46
   f. Mark 1:35

2. Read Matthew 16:24–28 and Luke 9:23–27. How often are we to "take up our cross" and follow Jesus?

3. How often did God provide manna for the Israelites wandering in the desert? (Exodus 16:4–5)

4. What does Jesus call Himself in John 6:35?

5. Why were the disciples unable to cast out the demon in the following two accounts of the same incident? (Mark 9:25–29; Matthew 17:14–21)

6. How do you think time spent in prayer strengthens our faith?

7. Let's spend some time examining Moses and his encounters with God.
   a. Read Exodus 20:19–20. What was the Israelites' emotional response when God spoke directly to them?
   b. What did they say to Moses?
   c. On the other hand, how anxious was Moses to have God speak to him? (Exodus 34:28)
   d. How did God speak to Moses? (Exodus 33:11)
   e. What was Moses' request? (Exodus 33:13)
   f. Moses also wanted to see God's glory. In order to prevent Moses from seeing God's face, where was he hidden? (Exodus 33:21–22)
   g. Where are you, as a child of God, now hidden? (Colossians 3:3)
   h. What is Jesus called in 1 Corinthians 10:4?
   i. What was the outward result of Moses' time at God's spa? (Exodus 34:29–30)

8. How does Jesus still speak to us today? (John 10:27)

9. One way He speaks to us is through His Word. What does each of these verses say about the Word of God?
   a. Hebrews 4:12
   b. 2 Peter 1:19–21
   c. 2 Timothy 3:16–17
   d. Matthew 5:17–18

◆ ◆

LESSON TWELVE

As we close this study, I want us to focus on Jesus' parting words to His disciples and to us. Imagine a soldier going off to war. He knows he will be placed on the front line of battle. The week before he's dispatched, he sits down to write his wife one final letter. He tries to include the essentials—how to continue in his absence, how to resist discouragement, and how much he loves and cherishes her. This is the scene of John 14 through 17 as Jesus reveals His heart to the Twelve before He goes to the final battle at the Cross.

Read John 14 and either mark or list every word of instruction or encouragement, then answer the following:
   1. Why should we not let our hearts be troubled?

   2. Where was Jesus going, and why was He going there?

   3. How does a person get to the Father?

   4. How does someone know what the Father is like?

   5. Where did Jesus' words come from?

   6. According to verse 12, what kinds of works is a Christian able to do?

   7. What promise does Jesus make in verses 13 and 14?

   8. How do we prove we love Jesus? (vv. 15, 21, 23, 24)

   9. Whom did Jesus send to be with us? (vv. 16–17)

10. What are some names for the Holy Spirit?

11. What kind of hold did the prince of the world have on Jesus? (v. 30)

12. Why did Jesus go to the Cross? (v. 31)

13. Read John 15:1–11 and note everything you learn about *remaining* or *abiding* in Christ.

14. Read John 17 and note what Jesus prayed for Christians then and now. How do we know His prayer is for us today?

15. Write a prayer of praise for what God has done in your life through this study.

"There is no beautifier of complexion, or form, or behavior, like the wish to scatter joy and not pain around us."

—Virgil

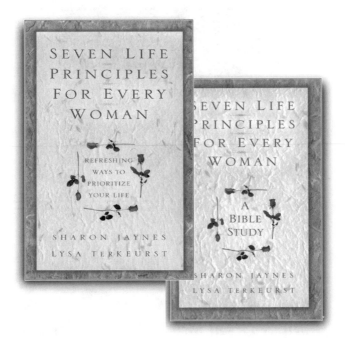

Seven Life Principles for Every Woman

- Book and Bible Study -

In our modern culture, boundaries are blurred, roles are reversed and priorities are perplexing. Using the principles of the Proverbs 31 woman, Sharon Jaynes and Lysa TerKeurst invite you to dive into God's Word and learn refreshing ways to prioritize your life. This book is written for all women -- professional, homemakers, wives, mothers, and grandmothers. There is also a Bible Study Guide which offers two lessons for each of the seven principles. The studies will help you seek the Lord for ways to keep your priorities in order and be all that He has created you to be.

ISBN: 0-8024-3398-7 Seven Life Principles
ISBN: 0-8024-3397-9 Seven Life Principles Bible Study

Parenting Helps from Sharon Jaynes and Moody Publishers

Being a Great Mom, Raising Great Kids

- Her children rise up and call her blessed -

What is every mother's heart's desire? Of course, it's to be a great Mom and raise great kids. But what does that mean and how can you achieve such a result? In *Being a Great Mom, Raising Great Kids*, she presents seven key attributes of a godly mother gleaned from Proverbs 31.

"Sharon has provided just the motivation and inspiration moms need to become women of Proverbs 31."

- Beverly LaHaye, Founder & Chairman of Concerned Women for America.

ISBN: 0-8024-6531-5

MOODY
PUBLISHERS
THE NAME YOU CAN TRUST.

1-800-678-6928 www.MoodyPublishers.org

Since 1894, Moody Publishers has been dedicated to equip and motivate people to advance the cause of Christ by publishing evangelical Christian literature and other media for all ages, around the world. As a ministry of the Moody Bible Institute of Chicago, proceeds from the sale of this book help to train the next generation of Christian leaders.

If we may serve you in any way in your spiritual journey toward understanding Christ and the Christian life, please contact us at www.moodypublishers.com.

"All Scripture is God-breathed and is useful for teaching, rebuking, correcting and training in righteousness, so that the man of God may be thoroughly equipped for every good work."
—2 TIMOTHY 3:16, 17

MOODY
PUBLISHERS

THE NAME YOU CAN TRUST

Date Due

Code 4386-04, CLS-4, Broadman Supplies, Nashville, Tenn.,
Printed in U.S.A.